Everyone Can Quilt

with Kaye Wood

100+ Tips, Techniques, Templates & Projects

©2004 Kaye Wood

Published by

kp **krause publications**
An imprint of F+W Publications, Inc.

700 East State Street • Iola, WI 54990-0001
715-445-2214 • 888-457-2873
www.krause.com

Our toll-free number to place an order or obtain a free catalog is 800-258-0929.

Quilts machine quilted by Annette Kimball, West Branch, Michigan,
and Cynthia Smith, Phoenix, Arizona.

Library of Congress Catalog Number: 2004093066

ISBN: 0-87349-812-7

Edited by Nicole Gould
Designed by Donna Mummery

Printed in the United States of America

Kaye Wood—
A teacher by choice! A quilt teacher by chance!

When I grow up, I want to be a teacher. My passion is teaching.

I have taught swimming, lifesaving, canoeing, outdoor cooking, leadership training courses, typing, and shorthand.

With four preschoolers (the fifth child was yet to be born), I started taking sewing classes to maintain my sanity. I wanted to get in the playpen and let them have the run of the house. But that didn't work, so I learned to sew with one of them sitting in my lap and another sitting on the foot pedal.

Soon I was hooked, and I took all the sewing classes available.

My teachers will tell you that the pressing part was not my favorite, but I did learn that the pressing techniques made a big difference in the final product. Now I stress the importance of accurate pressing in my quilt making.

A traveling teacher, Clotilde, came to our area. What was it about her that brought people to listen to her? What could I do to achieve that goal?

Of course, Clotilde is a good teacher and presenter, but more importantly, she specializes in one area of expertise.

I needed a specialty. You can't just find a specialty; a specialty finds you! In 1975, I started traveling and teaching free motion machine embroidery, and I felt that I was getting closer to a specialty.

And now for the "by chance" part.

One of my students asked if I would teach a quilting class. Why not? So I taught my first quilting class when I had never made a quilt, but the important part was that my students knew I was learning along with them.

I knew how to sew strips together, so we sewed strips. This was BRC (before rotary cutters), so we marked the strips and cut them with scissors, and simple designs were made. I knew how to press, so we pressed. Within six months, teaching quilting had taken over my life.

In the late '80s, I was taping videos to accompany some of my books. The producer said I should be on TV. Why not? I mortgaged our house and began my TV career with "Strip Quilting," then "Quilting for the '90s," then "Kaye's Quilting Friends."

More than 20 years later, we have 13 grandchildren, and I am still stripping in more than 30 books and patterns and over 500 TV programs.

After one of my seminars, a student said, "You are a quilt engineer." I thought, "She is right." The part of quilting I enjoy the most is the math, mostly geometry, and making quilts easier to piece so my students can enjoy success.

But for my students, my techniques are mathless. Accuracy is built into the steps, pieces can be made any size, and there is very little wasted fabric.

Kaye Wood

Table of Contents

Chapter 1

Introduction

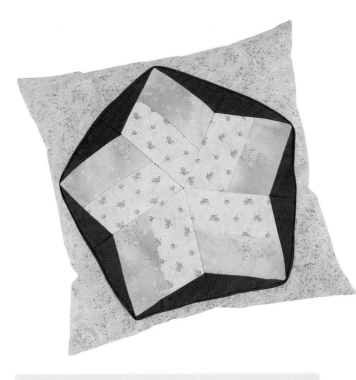

What kind of quilter are you?

Are you Pointed?

You are a Pointed Person if ...

❀ You like designs that have a lot of points and your points always match.

❀ You will tackle any quilt design and be reasonably sure that you can do it.

❀ You can eyeball ¼" without a ruler.

❀ You really believe you can teach anyone to match points.

❀ You have a love affair with a seam ripper.

❀ Your favorite stitch is the Frog Stitch (rip-it, rip-it).

A Great Gift Idea!
Buy your Pointed Friends a seam ripper—they always need another.

Or are you Pointless?

You are a Pointless Person if ...

❀ You don't like to match points.

❀ You don't care if your points match.

❀ You can't see well enough to match points.

❀ Your seam allowances wander, and it's okay with you.

❀ You would rather leave it than rip it out.

❀ You can say with a straight face, "My quilt is an artistic expression. I worked hard to get my points offset just a little."

I used to think I could teach anyone to match points, but my life won't be long enough, and some of you are not even trying!

Pointless People, you can come out of the closet and admit to being Pointless. But, if you want to remain a closet Pointless Person, choose one of my Pointless Projects.

If you are one of the Pointless People, treat your points like children. How? Separate the points (e.g., with sashing strips) or move them (to a different part of the quilt or turn them in a different direction).

But, if you want to be a Pointed Person and match your points, follow my step-by-step instructions for cutting, sewing, and pressing, and your points will be much easier to match.

How do I match seams and points?

Always use the easiest method that will work for the project and the fabric. These matching techniques are listed from the easiest to the most difficult.

Normal matching

Pinless
Seams interlock, see Chapter 3, page 30.
Fingerpin, see Chapter 3, page 30.
Needle Match, see Chapter 5, page 77.
Crease Mark, see Chapter 5, page 87 and Chapter 7, page 129.
60-degree Match, see Chapter 6, page 94.
Y-seam, see Chapter 6, page 96.

Pins
Diamond Match, see Chapter 6, page 108.

Basting Stitch
Set your machine for a long stitch. If your points match, sew over this stitching with a regular stitch length.

Desperation matching

Adhesive
Use double-faced ⅛" tape so you won't stitch over it.

1. Peel the paper off one side of the tape.

2. Cut a 1½" piece.

3. Stick it to the wrong side of the seam allowance at the point you want to match.

4. On the other piece, fold the seam allowance to the wrong side.

5. From the right side, put the pieces together with the points matching. The tape will hold the points in place.

6. Stitch the seamline. Remove the tape.

Sew over pins (*Did I really say that?*)
Use the needle up/needle down button or the handwheel to take one stitch at a time.

Hand stitch through points
Take a few hand stitches to hold the points together, and then machine stitch.

What supplies do I need to get started?

- ❀ Sewing machine
- ❀ Starmaker® 5, 6, and 8
- ❀ 6" x 24" ruler (most versatile)
- ❀ 6" x 12" ruler is also handy
- ❀ Rotary cutter and mat
- ❀ Static stickers to mark ruler
- ❀ Straight pins
- ❀ Iron (my choice is cordless)
- ❀ Fabric and batting

How much fabric do I buy?

A lot. Fabric is the palette I need to create a beautiful quilt. When the creative bug hits, I don't want to have to shop for fabric. It often hits in the middle of the night, and fabric shop owners would frown on being open. So, I feed my stash regularly, and I feed it well. I very rarely buy fabric for a particular quilt. Instead, I make my quilts from my stash. And guess what! Since I already have the fabric and I'm using up what I have, my quilt doesn't cost me any money. It's FREE!

The Fabric Police

There is a law that you cannot leave a state without buying fabric. Soon after I mentioned this in a seminar, I got a phone call from a man who said, "My wife was at your seminar and I understand there is a fabric law."

"Every quilter knows about this law," I said.

"Well, I'm a state trooper, and no one at the post knew about this law, but when we checked with our quilting wives, they all knew."

What fabrics do I buy to feed my stash?

- Color families (fabric with shades and tints of the same color). For example, all the blues would be in one color family.
- Colors that like each other.
- Accent colors (they make you say "Wow").

When planning my quilts, this formula sometimes helps:

70% medium shades
20% to 25% dark or light shades
5% to 10% accent colors.

How many UFOs do you have?

Some of you have a lot of UFOs (Un-Finished Objects); some have none; most of you have a few. Your personality type has a big influence on the way you approach your quilts.

If you have to finish one project before starting another, you have my sympathy. I like change, so I like to have several projects in the works; that way, I can work on whichever one talks to me that day.

I often hear "I will be so glad when this quilt is finished; then I never want to see it again."

News Alert!

Quilting is supposed to be fun and a stress reliever. My philosophical thought for the day:

Some quilts do not deserve to be finished!

What part of quilt making do you like?

Since this is supposed to be fun, you don't have to do it all. Each part of quilt making takes different skills and thought processes, and you may want to partner with someone to work on a quilt.

I enjoy the planning and the piecing of the quilt top, so that is what I do. I send all of my quilts out to be machine quilted by someone who likes to do the quilting.

Designing a quilt can be done in a variety of ways. I start with a particular technique, such as cutting diamonds. Some of you let the fabric direct you; some make a pattern that is already planned.

Starting a project takes a lot of thought: pattern and fabric choices, etc. When I'm in the starting mode, I start several projects.

Continuing a project takes attention to accuracy.

Finishing a project is like heaven to some of you; it's a sad ending to others of you.

Do I wash my fabric?

I usually do not wash my fabric unless there is a real reason for me to wash it.

Some valid reasons to wash fabric:

- If you plan to wash your quilted project.
- If you lose sleep about colors bleeding.
- If your fabric has too much sizing.
- If shrinking would be a problem.

If you decide not to wash your fabric, you have to be able to live with the above-mentioned problems.

If you wash your fabric, cut diagonally across each corner before washing. This will keep the edges from raveling.

Tip From A Quilting Friend:

Mary Jane Holcomb shared this tip with me:

If you want to wash a large piece of fabric, accordion-fold the fabric along one selvedge.

Pin the folds in place with large safety pins.

Hold the fabric by the pinned edge and let it hang.

The bottom selvedges will also fold; pin these.

Then wash and dry with no tangles.

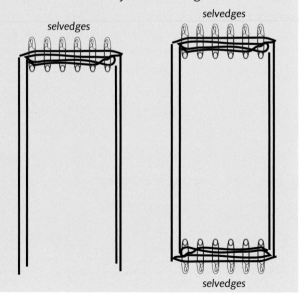

selvedges

selvedges

selvedges

What machine techniques are special?

Along my quilting road, I discovered that special techniques were needed for rotary cutting and machine sewing, some of which I developed* and some of which are general knowledge. Among those techniques are:

- ❀ Rotary cutting;
- ❀ Strip piecing to cut diamonds*;
- ❀ Starmaker Master Templates for accurate angles, any size*;
- ❀ Anchor seamlines*;
- ❀ Perfect Y-seams*;
- ❀ Finger pinning;
- ❀ Pinning with the grain line*;
- ❀ Starter Scraps (SS); and
- ❀ Sewing over seamlines.

Every step in my sewing and cutting techniques is a solution to a problem my students have had and will help you to easier and more successful patchwork.

Cutting Techniques

Cut Strips

Strips for most projects are cut cross grain (from selvedge to selvedge). These strips are a convenient length (42"/44") to use in your piecing.

The lengthwise grain has less stretch and is sometimes used for vertical (up and down) sashing and border strips.

Strips need to be cut straight

If the fold of the fabric is visible, cut at right angles to the fold. It's OK if the selvedges do not line up.

If the fold is no longer visible, fold the fabric in half with the selvedges together. Lay the fabric down and slide the top layer to one side until the fabric lays flat.

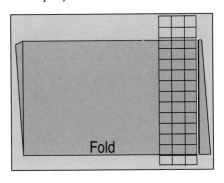

Straighten the fabric by cutting it at right angles to the fold. Do this by placing a cross line on a ruler on the fold, and then rotary cutting the fabric.

The shorter the distance to rotary cut, the easier it is to cut accurately; so after straightening the fabric, fold the fabric in fourths and cut strips, lining up a ruler with the folded edge.

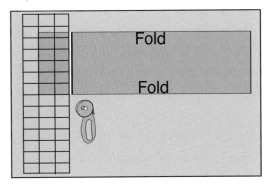

I like to undo one fold of the fabric and re-straighten the edge after cutting five or six strips. Then refold, restraighten, and continue cutting strips.

After a strip is cut, do an accuracy check.

Accuracy Tip:
Fold the cut strip in half, end to end. Is the strip the same width at both ends and at the center of the strip?

Straighten the strip or strip set

Before cutting squares or rectangles, trim the end of the strip or strip set to straighten and remove the selvedge.

If you are cutting the strips or strip sets for diamonds, don't bother to straighten the ends.

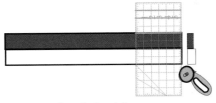

Diagram is for right-handed cutting.

Right-handed quilters, trim on the far right side. Left-handed quilters, trim on the far left side.

Sewing Techniques

There are special techniques that work for machine sewing. Use these instead of adapting hand-sewing techniques.

Seam Allowances

Use ¼" seam allowances for the projects in this book, unless otherwise noted. Some quilters like to use a full ¼" and some like a scant ¼" for a seam allowance. What is the difference? It's enough to change the size of your block or quilt. **But with the designs in this book, pick your seam allowance and stick with it.** Any seam allowance will work, but be sure to use the same seam allowance throughout the whole project.

Use some kind of a guide, such as a ¼" foot made for your sewing machine, to keep your seam allowances all the same. There also are other guides and gadgets available.

Anchor Seams

Anchor is a term I use for my technique of sewing the seamlines all the way from one edge to the next. Anchored seams eliminate problems when piecing diamonds and stars.

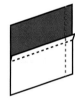

New seamlines are shown in red.

Starter Scrap (SS)

A Starter Scrap is a small scrap of fabric used to start and end a seam. Starter Scraps save thread, eliminate thread tails on your project, and keep the thread from jamming at the start of the seam.

But even more important, an SS will keep the points of the diamonds from distorting as you begin sewing the points together. Without an SS, the seam at the beginning and end of a strip tends to be narrower.

Lock Stitching

Lock Stitching is simply stitching in place to lock your stitch.

Pressing for accuracy

Pressing is different from ironing. Pressing is done in two different ways: an up-and-down motion to set the seams, and moving the iron with the grain line to press the seam allowances.

Pressing for accurate patchwork should be done:

1. WITHOUT steam. Steam can stretch and distort the fabric.
2. From the right side of the fabric. This will avoid pleats that form at the seamline.

Setting seams

This means pressing the seamline exactly as the seam was sewn. This sets the stitches in the middle of the fabric and makes a sharper seamline.

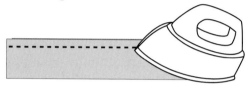

Rolling the strips

Pressing from the right side of the fabric can be done by rolling the strips.

1. Place the iron on the strip that will not have the seam allowances pressed toward it.

2. Hold the other strip or strips up in the air.

3. Move the iron from the first strip across to the other strips, unrolling the strips as you press across them.

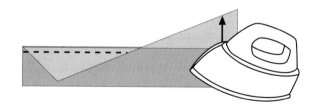

Once the seams are pressed in one direction, make sure they stay in that direction during the sewing process.

Sometimes my techniques call for the direction of the seam allowance to be temporarily changed to help match seams; but, before sewing, the seam allowance is returned to its pressed direction.

Chapter 2

No-Problem Quilts

If you have cruised to the Caribbean, you have probably heard someone say, "No problem, mon."

When I heard this in response to a question I asked, I thought it meant that I didn't have to worry and that they would take care of it for me.

No, that's not what it means. It means, "They don't care, and why should you."

But how does this apply to a quilt pattern?

Sometimes we need to de-stress our lives, and a No-Problem pattern can help us to do that. It means that there is virtually nothing you can do wrong while doing the next quilts.

They are called "No-Problem Quilts."

Size: 47" x 65"
by Emily Quinlan
Emily used flannel for her very first quilt.

Emily's Quilt

This is a great Pointless Project because there are no points to match and your seam allowances don't have to be perfect. It also is fun for using up your scraps or fat quarters. Make a memory quilt: Take this colorful, fun quilt to school or camp and have your friends autograph the blocks.

Yardage

⅓ yd. each of 10 different fabrics for rectangles

1⅔ yd. for sashing and borders

4 yd. for backing

52" x 70" piece of batting

⅔ yd. for binding

Quilting Cruises

I have been fortunate enough to take quilters on a cruise once or twice a year. We have classes, lectures, and sharing while at sea. In the ports, we are free to shop or take the tours. Here are some of the funny things that have happened while we have cruised. My friend Jane Hill, from Boca Raton, FL, has been with me on most of the quilting cruises. You'll read more about Jane later.

"George" the Quilter

One of the quilting cruisers came to dinner carrying a small box.

I asked, "What's in the box?" She said, "It's George." I knew I should not have asked. Carrying on, I said, "George must have really liked to cruise." She said, "George would never go on a cruise, George would never let me cruise, and George did not like quilters or quilts. Now George goes on a quilting cruise twice a year."

So George came to every meal and every class. We all said, "Hi, George." His box was featured on a quilt in the center of our group pictures.

Sew the rectangles into rows.

1. Cut 144 rectangles 3" x 5½". If several rectangles of the same color are used, first cut a 3" wide strip, and then cut this strip into 5½" pieces.

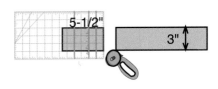

2. Start on a Starter Scrap (SS) and sew two rectangles, right sides together.

3. Chain stitch to the next set of rectangles and continue sewing. Chain stitching saves thread and speeds up the sewing process.

4. Sew the two rectangles into groups of four, eight, etc.

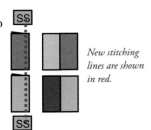

New stitching lines are shown in red.

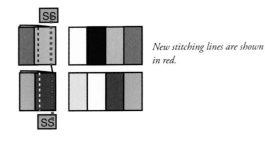

New stitching lines are shown in red.

5. Continue sewing until each row has 24 rectangles. There are six rows in this quilt.

6. Set the seams. Press the seam allowances all in one direction. (See Chapter 1 for directions on setting seams and pressing for accuracy.)

7. If the ends of the pieces do not line up perfectly, trim one or both sides.

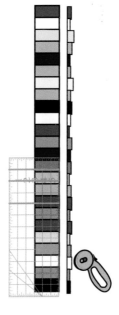

Measure the length of the rows.

Are all of your rows the same length? The length of the rows is the measurement needed to cut each of the sashing strips.

1. Lay the strips on top of each other to check for length. Use this length to cut the sashing strips.

2. If the lengths are different, trim a little off both the top and bottom of the longer strips so the lengths are all the same.

Cut the sashing strips.

1. Cut 10 strips, 3" wide.

2. Sew two strips together to make five long sashing strips.

3. Press the seam allowances open.

4. Cut these strips the same length as the rows.

5. I think these sashing strips look best if the seamline is in the middle of the strip. Start from the center and measure half the length of the quilt strips on each side of the center seam.

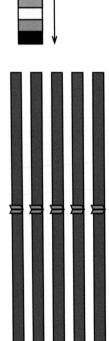

Pin a sashing strip to each row.

A sashing strip goes to the right-hand side of five of the rows of blocks.

1. Match and pin the top and bottom of each row of rectangles with the top and bottom of the sashing strips.

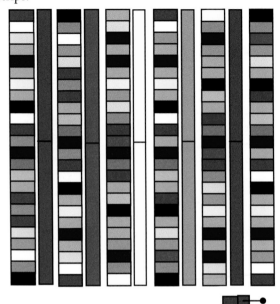

2. Place a pin even with the center seam on the sashing strip and the center of the row. Use as many pins as needed to evenly distribute the row along the sashing strip.

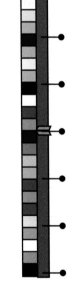

In the Quilter's Dream World, the rows would all be the same length. But we live in the Real World. The rows may not be the same length, and that's OK. Since quilting is supposed to be fun, and ripping out is not fun, we are NOT going to rip things out!

For this quilt, trim the longer strips so all strips are all the same length. Trim an equal amount from the top and bottom of each strip. BUT, to help improve your skills, there are reasons why the rows may not be the same length:

• Were the strips all cut the same width and cut accurately?
• Were the seam allowances all the same?
• Did you press without steam, from the right side of the fabric?

Re-read Chapter 1 about cutting, sewing, and pressing accurately.

Sew a sashing strip to each row.

Keep your quilt square: Make the quilt fit the sashing strip!

The measured sashing strip is the correct length of the quilt. The row should fit. If necessary, the row can be pulled a little taut or eased in slightly when sewing so it will fit the sashing strip.

1. Sew with the sashing strip on top.

2. Sew from pin to pin, holding the sashing strip taut at the next pin. Do not sew over the pins, but remove each pin as you come close to it.

3. Set the seams; see Chapter 1. This will set the stitches in the middle of the seamline and make it easier to press accurately. Press the seam allowances toward the sashing strip.

Sew the rows together.

1. Pin the sashing strip to the next row of rectangles, matching the top and bottom.

2. Use as many pins as needed to evenly distribute the row along the sashing strip.

3. Sew the rows together with the sashing strip on top to control stretching. Sew from pin to pin, holding the sashing strip taut to ease in the row. Do not sew over the pins, but remove each of these pins as you come close to it.

4. Set the seams. Press the seam allowances toward the sashing strips.

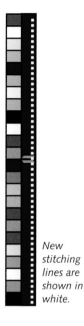

New stitching lines are shown in white.

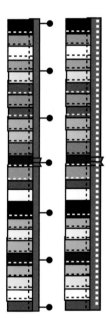

New stitching lines are shown in white.

Borders:
Top and Bottom

Keep your quilt square: Make the quilt fit the border!

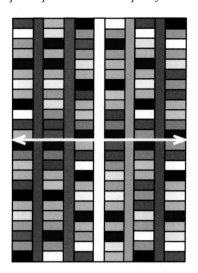

1. Measure the width of the quilt across the center.

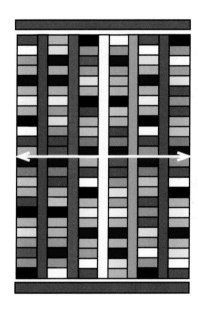

2. Cut two 3" wide strips the length needed for the borders.

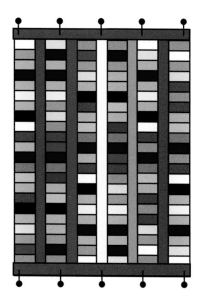

Borders: Side
Keep your quilt square: Make the quilt fit the border!
If a quilt is to be hung on the wall, it is better to cut the side borders from the length of the fabric instead of across the width of the fabric (from selvedge to selvedge).

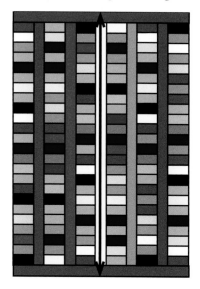

3. Find the center of the border strip by folding it in half, end to end. Match the center on the sashing strip to the center of the rows and the ends of the rows. Use as many pins as necessary to ease the quilt to fit the border strip.

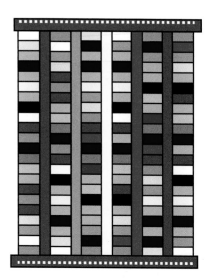

4. Sew a border strip to the top and bottom of the quilt, right sides together, with the border strip on top. Sew from pin to pin, holding the border strip taut to ease in the row. Do not sew over the pins. Remove each pin as you come close to it.

5. Set the seams. Press the seam allowances toward the border strip. (See Chapter 1 for directions on setting seams and pressing for accuracy.)

1. Measure the length of the quilt in the center, including the top and bottom borders.

2. Cut four 3"-wide strips the length needed for the borders.

3. Sew two strips together to make them long enough for the quilt.

4. Press the seam allowances open.

5. Match the center seam and the ends of the sashing strip to the center of the rows and the ends of the rows. Use as many pins as necessary to ease the quilt to fit the border strip.

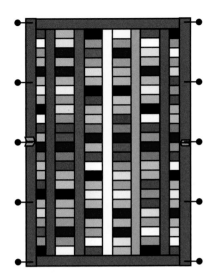

6. Sew a border strip to the quilt, right sides together, with the border strip on top. Sew from pin to pin, holding the border strip taut to ease in the row. Do not sew over the pins. Remove each pin as you come close to it.

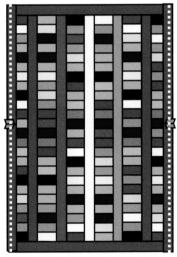

New stitching lines are shown in white.

7. Set the seams, and then press the seam allowances toward the border strip. (See Chapter 1 for directions on setting seams and pressing for accuracy.)

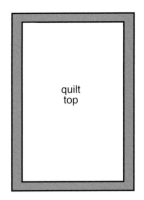

Finish the quilt.

1. Layer the quilt. Machine quilt, hand quilt, or tie.

2. After quilting or tying the quilt, trim the backing fabric so it is 1" larger than the quilt on all four sides. (The 1" will wrap around to the front to make a ½" finished binding.)

3. Trim the batting even with the quilt top.

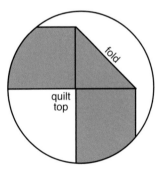

4. Fold and press the corners of the backing to the corners of the quilt top.

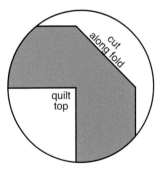

5. Cut the corner of the backing off along the fold line.

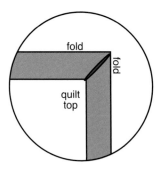

6. Fold and press all sides of the backing to the edge of the quilt top.

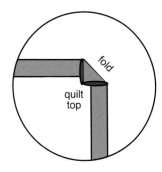

7. Fold the corner of the backing to the corner of the quilt.

8. Fold the backing again to cover the edge of the quilt. Pin the binding in place.

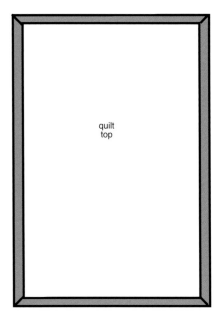

9. Topstitch with a straight or decorative stitch close to the edge of the binding.

Mixed Bricks Quilt

This is a great Pointless Project! There is just no way the seams can match, even if you try.

Yardage

Make this quilt any size. Because scraps are used, no yardages are given. But if you buy fabric for this quilt top:

Twin:	total of 6 yd.
Double:	total of 8 yd.
Queen:	total of 10 yd.
King:	total of 12 yd.

Cut the pieces.

The pieces can be any length, but all of the pieces in one row have to be the same width. For instance, in one row all of the pieces might be cut 2" wide. In another row, they might be cut 3" or 4" wide. This quilt looks best if the lengths of each of the pieces vary, which is a real bonus for the Pointless People: There is no way the seams can match, so don't try.

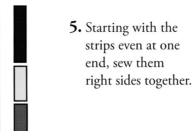

Sew the rows.

1. Sew the same width pieces, right sides together, into a strip long enough for your bed. The strips can go across or lengthwise on the bed.

2. As the strips get longer, take them to the bed to see if the strips are long enough. If not, add more pieces.

3. Make all the strips approximately the same length. They will be trimmed square after they are sewn together.

4. Press the seam allowances all in the same direction.

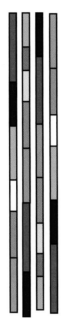

5. Starting with the strips even at one end, sew them right sides together.

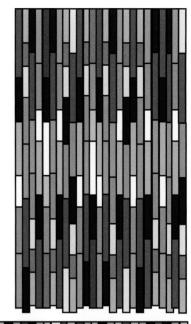

6. Square up the top and bottom edges.

Finish the quilt.

1. Layer the quilt. Machine quilt, hand quilt, or tie.

2. Bring the backing around to the front to form a binding (see Emily's Quilt, page 17).

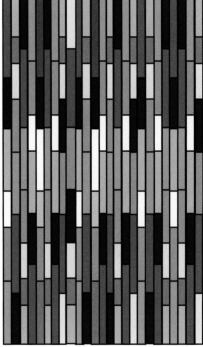

My "Free" Quilt

I use leftover pieces from some of my other projects, so the fabric is really "free."

As I work on projects, I cut small leftover pieces into 2", 3", or 4" wide pieces, all different lengths. I also save extra strips that have been cut, which I cut into lengths from 4" to 10".

I sew the same width strips (all 2" or all 3", etc.) into a long strip, roll the strip up, and put a rubber band around it. More pieces are added to the roll as I finish each project.

When I want to make a No-Problem Scrap Quilt, I cut the lengths that I need from the roll.

Any kind of fabric works well; even those double knits you can't stand to throw away can be used. Cottons, poly-cotton, denim, or flannel also are good choices.

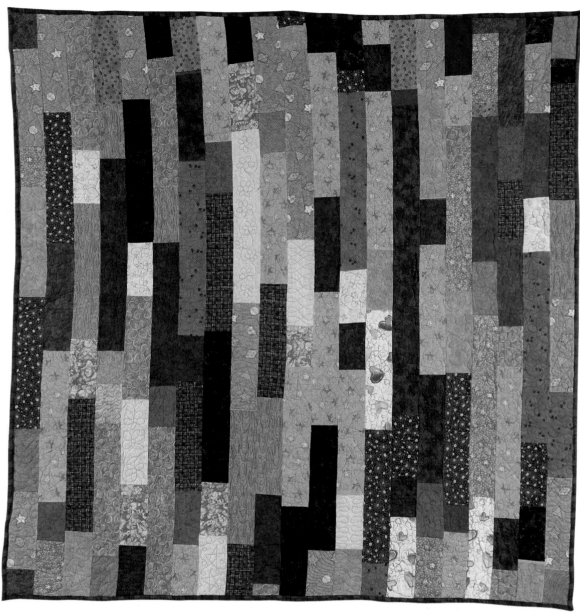

Try Some Innovative Ideas To Quilt The Layers Together

Make square pockets; topstitch around three sides of the pocket. Things can be put into the pockets.

If the quilt is made from used bluejeans, quilt it by topstitching through the jean pockets, belt loops, or labels.

This quilt is great for picnics or for the beach.

If I were into quilts for pets, as some of you are, this would be my choice.

Chapter 3

Rail Fence and Pinwheel Quilts

Traditional quilt blocks, such as the Rail Fence and Pinwheel, can be made using contemporary piecing methods.

Experiment with color choices by making pot holders or place mats. If, for some reason, your colors don't "work," someone will like them. Give them away to the first person who admires them.

Size: 12" x 16"

To find the rail fence, follow either the dark or light fabric.

Rail Fence Place Mats

Make four identical place mats. Or for a fun casual table, choose just one fabric to keep constant in every place mat and choose different colors for the second fabric. Make your rectangle squares from as few as two strips per square to as many strips as you want.

Yardage: 4 place mats

1 yd. of each fabric for rectangle squares

1 yd. for backing

4 pieces (12" x 16") of batting

Sew strip sets.

1. Cut six 2½" x 42/44" strips from each fabric.

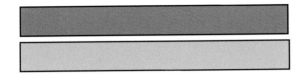

2. Sew six strip sets as shown.

3. Set the seams. Press the seam allowances toward the darker fabric. (See Chapter 1 for directions on setting seams and pressing for accuracy.)

Cut segments.

1. Mark a ruler the width of the entire strip set (approximately 4½") using tape or a piece of static sticker.

Accuracy Tip

This is the measurement used to cut the strip into rectangle squares.

2. Straighten the strip set. Refer to Chapter 1 for more information on straightening the strip set.

3. Place the ruler on the strip so the mark on the ruler lines up with the end of the strip set. A crossline on the ruler should be on the seamline to help keep the block square.

4. Cut one segment along the right-hand side of the ruler.

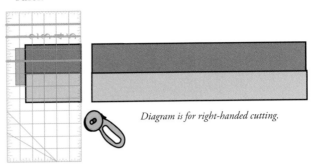

Diagram is for right-handed cutting.

Accuracy Check

Fold the segment diagonally. The corners should line up perfectly. If the corners do not line up, re-measure and re-mark the strip set width on the ruler. If the corners do line up, you have a perfect square. Congratulations!

5. Continue cutting 48 segments.

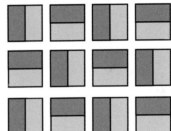

Sew into rows.

1. Lay out the segments for each place mat in the following rows:

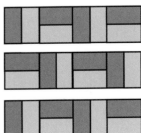

2. Sew into rows, matching the top and bottom of the segments.

3. Set the seams. Press the seam allowances toward the solid strip (away from the cross seam). (See Chapter 1 for directions on setting seams and pressing for accuracy.)

4. Sew the rows together. (Refer to the following pages for tips on matching seamlines.)

Finish the place mats.
Finish with an envelope style finish; see the A Step Above Quilt on page 32. Or layer and quilt the place mats and finish them with a binding strip.

San Blas Islands

The Cuna Indians of the San Blas Islands have some interesting traditions.

Airport

Each family lives on its own island. The shopping island, which is only used when the cruisers come to visit, had two things that were really interesting to me: an airport and a blue hut on the dock.

The island is very small, and only very small airplanes can land at the airport. The control tower is a bamboo tower. If the plane misses the really short runway, it will be in the water.

Money, Money, Money

The Cuna Indians are known for molas, which they bring to their shopping island for the cruisers.

As our ship arrived, the Cunas paddled their dugout canoes to the cruise ship. These primitive people have really figured this cruise business out. They shouted "money, money, money" and we all threw money to them. What a concept.

Some of the coins went in the upside down umbrellas they used, but some money went into the water. So these primitive Indians put on their fins and masks and dove for the money.

The Chief

We were lucky enough to meet with Danny, the chief. At least, he told us he was the chief. I asked Danny how he came to be the chief. He said because he had been to Panama. Boy, was I impressed — until later in the day. We realized that the San Blas Islands were a part of Panama. Because he is the chief, Danny charged us $2 to have our picture taken with him.

Rail Fence Squares

All strips are 42/44" long.

Segment Size	Block Width	Strip Width	Segments per Strip Set
2½" x 2½"	1½"	2½"	16
3½" x 3½"	2"	3½"	12
4½" x 4½"	2½"	4½"	9
5½" x 5½"	3"	5½"	7
6½" x 6½"	3½"	6½"	6

Adding Machine

Once on land, you can see all of the mola handwork hanging from clotheslines. These Indians have figured out that people will only buy a limited number of molas as a souvenir of the island. But, put the molas on a T-shirt, and every one of their friends has to have one.

The shopper, Jane, had a pile of about 35 molas. The Cuna woman handling Jane's sales added the numbers by writing the dollar amount of each item in the sand. When she had listed six or seven items, she ran out of sand. So she added those up, put the total at the top, erased the previous list, and continued adding items. Jane's total came to way over $200.

Even a sale like that didn't warrant a picture with this woman; that costs $1. But if Jane wanted a picture of the small pig nearby, that was only 10 cents.

Blue Hut

The blue hut on the dock is the outhouse. It has a hole that empties right into the water. I asked about pollution, but they assured me that they swam on the other side of the island and the currents ran away from the island.

Size: 40" x 70"

Rail Fence Quilt

The perfect quilt for a beginner, this two-color quilt will be completed in no time at all.

Yardage

1 yd. of each fabric for the rectangle squares
2/3 yd. for the first border
2/3 yd. for the second border
44" x 74" piece of fabric for the backing
44" x 74" piece of batting

Rail Fence Quilt Yardages

Quilt sizes are without borders. All strips are 42"/44" long.

Quilt Size	Strip Width	Strip Set Width*	Segments per Strip	Block Size**	Yardage for 72 rectangle squares***	Yardage for Each Border
12" x 24"	1½"	2½"	16	2½" x 2½"	¼ yd.	5"
18" x 36"	2"	3½"	12	3½" x 3½"	⅓ yd.	¼ yd.
24" x 48"	2½"	4½"	9	4½" x 4½"	⅔ yd.	½ yd.
30" x 60"	3"	5½"	7	5½" x 5½"	1 yd.	⅔ yd.
36" x 72"	3½"	6½"	6	6½" x 6½"	1¼ yd.	⅔ yd.
42" x 84"	4"	7½"	4	7½" x 7½"	2 yd.	½ yd.

*If your strip set measures more or less, use your measurement to mark the ruler and cut the segments.

**If your block size measures more or less, use your measurement to cut strips for the solid blocks.

***This yardage is needed for each of the two fabrics.

Sew strip sets.

1. Cut 11 3" x 42" strips from each of the rectangle square fabrics.

2. Sew 11 strip sets following the directions for making rectangle squares on page 25.

Cut segments.

1. Mark the width of the entire strip set (approximately 5½") on a ruler using tape or a piece of static sticker.

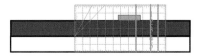

2. Cut 72 rectangle squares. Follow the directions for cutting rectangle squares on page 25.

Sew into rows.

1. Lay out the segments in the following rows:

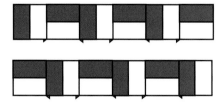

2. Sew into rows, matching the top and bottom of the segments.

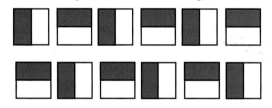

3. Set the seams. Press the seam allowances toward the solid strip, away from the cross seam. (See Chapter 1 for directions on setting seams and pressing for accuracy.)

Match the seams.

1. With right sides together, match the seamlines. The seam allowances should be going in opposite directions at each seamline, because each seam allowance was pressed toward the solid strip. Some of the seams interlock.

2. An interlocking seam is easy to match. The top seam allowance is toward the needle (away from you). The bottom seam allowance is toward you. Your sewing machine will help you match interlocking seams.

3. As you sew, finger pin (hold the matching seamlines together). The machine pushes the top seam into the center of the bottom seam and locks it into place.

4. Some of the seams do not interlock. The top seam is toward you, and the bottom seam is toward the machine. As you sew, finger pin (hold the matching seamlines together) OR pin the seamlines together.

Finger pin: Hold the two seamlines together with your fingers until the needle is close to the seam. Remove your fingers before sewing over the seam. Do not sew over your fingers as that would be painful.

Pin: Put the pin into the seamline on the top fabric, through to the seamline on the bottom fabric. Bring the pin up through the bottom seamline to the top seamline. Do not sew over pins. Instead, remove each pin as the needle approaches it.

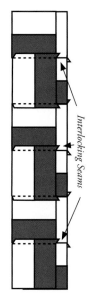

Interlocking Seams

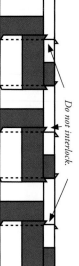

Do not interlock.

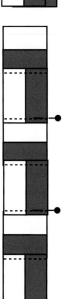

Sew the rows together.

1. Sew right sides together. You might want to start stitching on a Starter Scrap (see Chapter 1).

2. Set the seams. Press the seam allowances all in one direction. (See Chapter 1 for directions on setting seams and pressing for accuracy.)

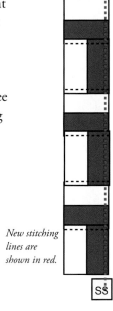

New stitching lines are shown in red.

First borders

1. Cut six 3" x 42" strips from the first border fabric. One strip will be used for the top border, one for the bottom border, and two strips for each of the side borders.

2. Top and bottom borders: Follow the instructions for cutting, sewing, and pressing top and bottom border strips given with Emily's Quilt on pages 15-16.

3. Side borders: Sew two strips together for each side border to make the strip long enough. Follow the instructions for cutting, sewing, and pressing side border strips given with Emily's Quilt on pages 15-16.

Second borders
1. Cut six 3" x 42" strips from the second border fabric.
2. Repeat the instructions above.

Finish the quilt.
Use an envelope finish. See the A Step Above Quilt on page 32 for directions.

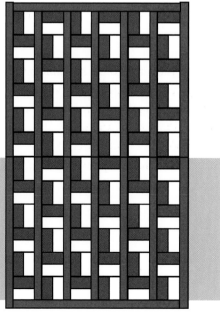

Size: 52" x 70"

Pointless Rail Fence Quilt
Try this quilt. It's a great Pointless design.

Sashing strips are added between each of the rows.

Sashing strips: 1 yard of fabric cut into 10 strips (3" x 42"). Two strips are sewn together for each sashing strip.

Measure the sashing strips, following the directions for Emily's Quilt on page 14.

Size: 37" x 56"

A Step Above Quilt

This Rail Fence Quilt has the added interest of a third fabric. This quilt is made from two different rectangle squares, one with dark/light fabrics and one with medium/light colored fabrics.

Yardage

For the rectangle squares:
1⅛ yd. light fabric
⅔ yd. medium fabric
⅔ yd. dark fabric
⅔ yd. for the first border
⅔ yd. for the second border
41" x 74" piece of fabric for the backing
41" x 74" piece of batting

Cut the strips.

1. From the light-colored fabric, cut 12 strips (3" x 42").

2. From the medium-colored fabric, cut six strips (3" x 42").

3. From the dark-colored fabric, cut six strips (3" x 42").

Sew strip sets.

1. Sew six strip sets with the light and medium fabrics.

2. Sew six strip sets with the light and dark fabrics.

3. The strip set width will be approximately 5½". Measure your strip set and use this measurement to mark a ruler and cut the segments.

Cut rectangle squares.

1. Cut 36 segments from the light/medium strip sets.

2. Cut 36 segments from the light/dark strip sets.

3. Follow the directions for cutting rectangle squares on page 25.

Sew the rows.

1. Sew the segments into rows, following the sewing instructions for the Rail Fence Quilt on page 29.

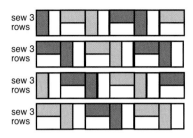

2. Sew the rows together, following the instructions for matching seamlines on page 30.

First borders

1. Cut four strips (3" x 42") from the first border fabrics.

2. Top and bottom borders: Follow the instructions for cutting, sewing, and pressing top and bottom border strips given with Emily's Quilt on page 15.

3. Side borders: Sew two strips together for each side border to make the strip long enough. Follow the instructions for cutting, sewing, and pressing side border strips given with Emily's Quilt on pages 15-16.

Second borders

1. Cut four strips (3" x 24") from the second border fabric.

2. Repeat the instructions above.

Finish the quilt.

Use an envelope-style finish:

1. Cut a piece of backing fabric 2" larger than the quilt top.

2. Cut a piece of batting 2" larger than the quilt top.

3. Carefully pin the quilt top and backing, right sides together, with the batting underneath.

4. Mark the start and stop spots with crossed pins. You'll know when to stop when you come to the crossed pins.

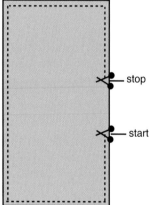

5. Sew around 3½ sides, from the starting to the stopping pins. Trim the backing and batting even with the quilt top.

6. Turn right side out.

7. Fold the edges of the opening to the inside.

8. Hand stitch the opening closed.

9. Machine quilt, hand quilt, or tie the quilt.

Bahamas

Shopping In The Water

There are water vendors who sell their wares from the water. Some of them carry their stuff; some drag a small boat filled with the stuff. They don't have licenses to sell on the land, so they walk up and down in the water near the shore, selling stuff to people like us.

Jane, the shopper, had to see all the wares, but made a classic mistake. She said to him, "It's too bad you don't take Visa, because I don't carry money in the water. Do you take credit cards?" (Does she carry her credit card in the water?)

He said, "I take Visa," as he pulled the credit card machine out of his hat.

Pinwheel Pot Holders

If you cook, these are pot holders; if you don't cook, they are kitchen quilts.

A pinwheel quilt block is made from four rectangle squares. Make two different pot holders with plain backs, or use one of the potholders for the front and one for the back.

The segments in each of the blocks are made the same, but the sewing steps are different.

Yardage

2 strips (2" x 18") of each fabric
2 strips (1¾" x 6") for hanging loops
2 pieces (7" x 7") batting*
Insul-Bright™ batting by the Warm™ Company is made especially for pot holders.

Pinwheel Blocks

All strips are 42"/44" long.

Block Size	Strip Width	Strip Set Width	Segments per Strip Set
4½" x 4½"	1½"	2½"	16
6½" x 6½"	2"	3½"	12
8½" x 8½"	2½"	4½"	9
10½" x 10½"	3"	5½"	7
12½" x 12½"	3½"	6½"	6

The project can be made from one light and one dark fat quarter.

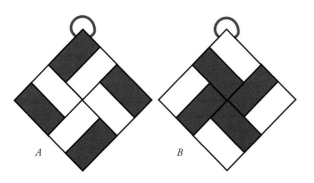

A   B

Sew strip sets.
1. Cut two strips (2" x 18") from each of the fabrics.

2. Sew the strips right sides together into a strip set.

Cut segments
1. Mark a ruler the width of the entire strip set (approximately 3½") using tape or a piece of static sticker.

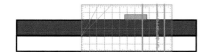

2. Straighten the strip sets, referring to page 9 for information.
3. Cut four segments for each pinwheel.

Follow the directions for cutting rectangle squares on page 25.

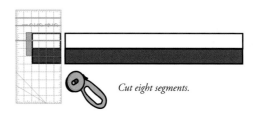

Cut eight segments.

Sew the rectangle squares into two rows.

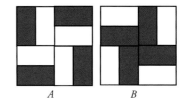

A   B

1. Pinwheel A: Line up two A segments, right sides together, with a horizontal seamline on top.

2. Pinwheel B: Line up two B segments, right sides together, with a vertical seamline on top.

3. Starting with a Starter Scrap, chainstitch the segments together:

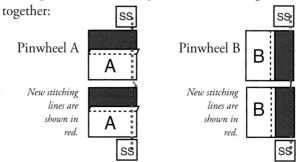

Pinwheel A   Pinwheel B

New stitching lines are shown in red.   *New stitching lines are shown in red.*

4. Set the seams. Press the seam allowances toward the solid strip (away from the cross seam). See Chapter 1 for directions on setting seams and pressing for accuracy.

Sew the rows together.

1. Line up the rows.

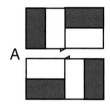 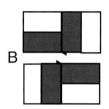
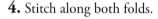

2. Starting with a Starter Scrap (SS), sew the two rows, right sides together, matching seamlines.

Pinwheel A: Line up the rows. The seamlines go in opposite directions and interlock. An interlocking seam is easy to match. The top seam allowance is toward the needle (away from you). The bottom seam allowance is toward you.

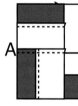

Your sewing machine will help you match interlocking seams. As you sew, hold the matching seamlines together. The machine pushes the top seam into the center of the bottom seam and locks it into place.

Pinwheel B: Line up the rows. The seamlines go in opposite directions, but do not interlock. The top seam is toward you and the bottom seam is toward the machine. These seams can be matched by finger pinning or by using pins.

 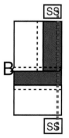

See Chapter 3, page 30, for directions on pinning and finger pinning.

3. Set the seams. Press the seam allowances in one direction.

Make the hanging tab.
1. Cut one strip of fabric (1¾" x 6") for each pot holder.

2. Fold the strip in half lengthwise, wrong sides together.

3. Open up and fold the raw edges into the center.

4. Stitch along both folds.

5. Fold the tab and sew both raw edges to the top of the potholder.

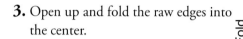
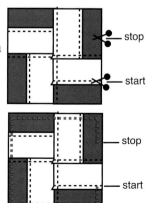

Envelope Finish
1. Cut a piece of batting the same size as the pinwheel block, approximately 6½" x 6½".

2. If the back of the potholder is a solid square, cut the backing square 6½" x 6½".

3. Place the two squares, right sides together, with the batting underneath.

4. Mark the start and stop spots with crossed pins. You'll know when to stop when you come to the crossed pins.

5. Sew around 3½ sides, from the starting to the stopping pins.

6. Turn right sides out.

7. Fold the edges of the opening to the inside.

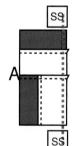

8. Hand stitch to close the opening or topstitch at ⅛" or ¼" with a straight or decorative stitch around the outside edges of the potholder.

Try arranging the rectangle squares in other designs.

Quilt the potholder.
If desired, sew over all of the seamlines with a decorative stitch.

Martinique

Shopping at the Topless Beach

No, Jane and I did not go topless!

But you should see the pictures that our husbands took while trying to be really casual and shooting from the hip as they walked along.

You actually can buy bathing suits at the beach. A saleswoman carried a basket full of bathing suits. If you picked out the suit you liked, she would take off her suit to model the one you picked out. Funny thing was, the suits were all made the same; the only difference was the color. And, the people picking out suits for her to model were mostly men. Go figure!

Famous Last Words: You'll Never See These People Again

We ran into two couples we recognized from the ship. It was very obvious that the women had not been topless before. They probably dared each other to do it by telling themselves that no one they knew would see them. Then we came along, and down under the water they went. We could have made them miss the ship if we had stayed there longer, but then we would have missed the ship, too.

Quilt made by Lori Jonsson
Size: 43" x 59"

Confetti Pinwheel Quilt

This quilt was made from all A blocks. A matching star pillow can be found on page 132.

Yardage

⅔ yd. of each fabric for the rectangle squares
¾ yd. for the solid blocks
½ yd. for the borders
47" x 63" piece of fabric for the backing
47" x 63" piece of batting
⅓ yd. for the binding

Pinwheel Quilt Yardages

Quilt sizes are without borders. All strips are 42"/44" long.

Quilt Size	Strip Width	Strip Set Width*	Segments per Strip Set	Pinwheel Block Size**	Yardage for 72 Segments***	Yardage for 17 Solid Blocks	Yardage for Binding
20" x 28"	1½"	2½"	16	4½" x 4½"	¼ yd.	⅓ yd.	5"
30" x 42"	2"	3½"	12	6½" x 6½"	⅓ yd.	½ yd.	¼ yd.
40" x 56"	2½"	4½"	9	8½" x 8½"	⅔ yd.	¾ yd.	¼ yd.
50" x 70"	3"	5½"	7	10½" x 10½"	1 yd.	⅔ yd.	⅓ yd.
60" x 84"	3½"	6½"	6	12½" x 12½"	1¼ yd.	¾ yd.	½ yd.

*If your strip set measures more or less, use your measurement to mark the ruler and cut the segments.

**If your block size measures more or less, use your measurement to cut strips for the solid blocks.

***This yardage is needed for each of the two fabrics.

Make the pinwheel quilt blocks.

1. Cut eight strips (2½" x 42"/44") from each of the pinwheel fabrics.

2. Sew the strip sets following the directions for making rectangle squares on the page 25.

3. Make 18 pinwheel A blocks. (72 rectangle squares.)

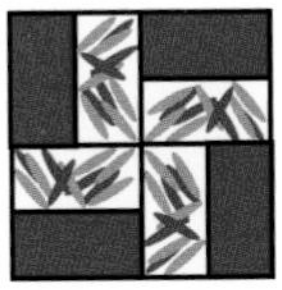

Cut the solid squares.

1. Mark the height of a pinwheel block (approximately 8½") on a ruler using tape or a piece of static sticker.

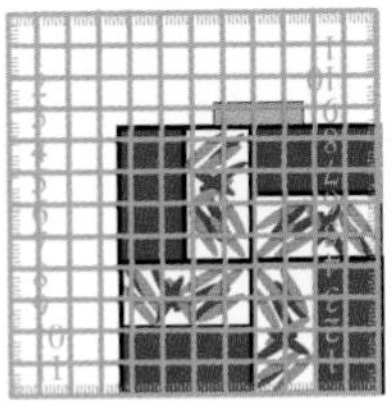

2. Cut two fabric strips the same width as your pinwheel block. For example, if your block size is 8½", cut the solid fabric into 8½" x 42" strips.

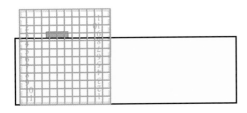

3. Cut these strips into 17 squares, using the marked ruler. For example, if the strips are 8½", cut the strip into 8½" squares.

Sew the pinwheel blocks into rows.

1. Alternate the pieced and solid blocks, following the quilt diagram.

2. Sew into rows, matching the top and bottom of each block.

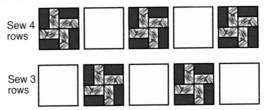

Sew 4 rows

Sew 3 rows

3. Set the seams. Press the seam allowances toward the solid-colored squares. (See Chapter 1 for directions on setting seams and pressing for accuracy.)

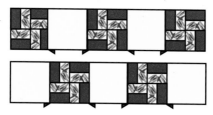

Sew the rows together.

1. Match the seamlines. Some seams interlock; some do not and must be finger-pinned or pinned. (See directions for the Rail Fence Quilt on page 30.)

2. Set the seams. Press all of the seam allowances in the same direction.

Finish the quilt.

1. Cut six strips (2" x 42") for the border.

2. Sew two strips together for each of the side borders. (See Emily's Quilt on page 15 for information on how to cut, measure, and sew the border strips.)

3. Layer the quilt (see page 137).

4. Hand or machine quilt.

5. Cut six binding strips (1¾" x 42").

6. Follow the instructions for applying the binding on pages 139-142.

Chapter 4

Nine-Patch Quilts

Nine-Patch quilt blocks refer to any block made from nine patches. In this chapter, some projects have nine squares and some are made from squares and rectangles.
Blocks can be put together with or without sashing strips.

Size: 7-1/2" x 7-1/2"

This would be a good fat quarter project! Use one light and one dark fat quarter.

Nine-Patch Pot Holders

A nine-patch block is made from nine squares. These potholders are turned "on point." Two different blocks can be made: one with the light-colored squares on the outside, and one with the dark-colored squares on the outside. Make two different potholders with plain backs or use one of the potholders for the front and the other for the back.

You also could create a quilt from all of one block or from both blocks.

Yardage: 2 pot holders

3 strips (3" x 12") of each fabric
8" x 8" piece of batting*

*Insul-Bright™ batting by the Warm™ Company is made especially for pot holders.

Nine-Patch Quilt Blocks

All strips are 42"/44".

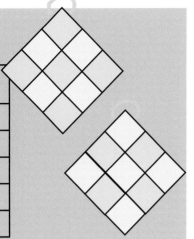

Block Size	Strip Width	Strip Set Width	Segments per Strip Set
3½" x 3½"	1½"	3½"	28
5" x 5"	2"	5"	21
6½" x 6½"	2½"	6½"	16
8" x 8"	3"	8"	14
9½" x 9½"	3½"	9½"	12

Sew strip sets.

1. For a 7½" pot holder, cut three strips (3" x 12") from each of the fabrics.

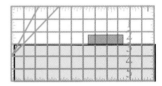

2. Mark a ruler at 3" (the width of one strip) using tape or a piece of static sticker.

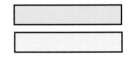

Accuracy Tip

This is the measurement used to cut the strip into segments.

3. Sew three strips together to form the A strip set.

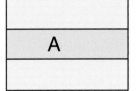

4. Sew three strips together to form the B strip set.

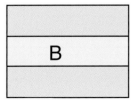

5. Set the seams. Press the seam allowances toward the darker fabric. (See Chapter 1 for directions on setting seams and pressing for accuracy.)

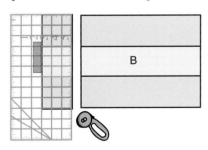

Cut segments.

1. Straighten the strip sets, referring to page 9 for information.

2. Place the ruler on the strip so the mark on the ruler lines up with the end of the strip set.

Accuracy Tip

Line up a cross line on the ruler with the seamline.

3. Cut three segments (3") from each of the strip sets.

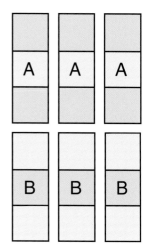

Sew the nine-patch blocks.

1. Line up an A and a B segment, right sides together.

2. Match the seamlines; one seamline will interlock, the other seamline needs to be pinned or finger pinned. (See page 30 for directions on pinning and finger pinning.)

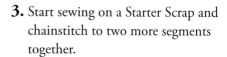

3. Start sewing on a Starter Scrap and chainstitch to two more segments together.

4. Add a B segment to the right side of one set as shown. Add an A segment to the left side of the other set as shown.

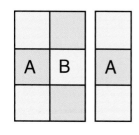
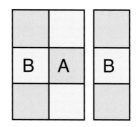

5. Line up the third segment, right sides together.

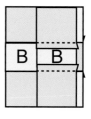

6. Start sewing on a Starter Scrap (SS), matching the seamlines. One seamline will interlock, the other needs to be pinned or finger pinned. (See page 30 for directions on pinning and finger pinning.) Sew all the way from the top to bottom, sewing off onto a Starter Scrap.

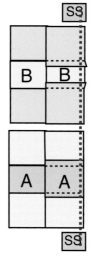

7. Set the seams. Press the seam allowances all in one direction.

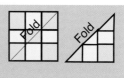

Accuracy Check

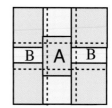

Fold the segment diagonally. The corners should line up perfectly.

If the corners do not line up, re-measure and re-mark the strip set width on the ruler.

Finish the potholders.

Refer to Pinwheel Potholders on page 38.

1. Make the hanging tab.

2. Cut a piece of batting the same size as the nine-patch block, approximately 8" x 8".

3. If the back of the potholder is a solid square, cut the backing square the same as the nine-patch.

4. Place the two nine-patch blocks (or one nine-patch and one solid square), right sides together, with the batting underneath.

5. Use an envelope finish (see page 38).

6. Sew decorative stitches over all of the seamlines to quilt the potholder.

In or Out

I was in the waiting room of my orthopedic surgeon waiting for a checkup after my knee replacement. There was a man waiting to get a cast off his leg. We started to chat, and of course we had to find out how each of us had been injured. He said he broke his leg in three places by kicking down the bedroom door.

"Were you trying to get in or get out of the bedroom?" is what I should have asked, but didn't really want to know.

Handicapped?

I taught in Denmark shortly after I had my cast removed after breaking all the bones and tearing all the ligaments in my ankle. I was still in a wheelchair some of the time.

Every time I had a question for the clerks at the front desk, they pointed me in the direction of the handicapped conference going on at the same time.

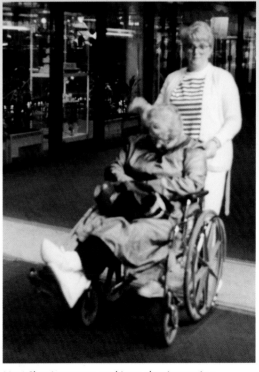

Meet Shar Jorgenson, pushing a sleeping me in a wheelchair in Amsterdam.

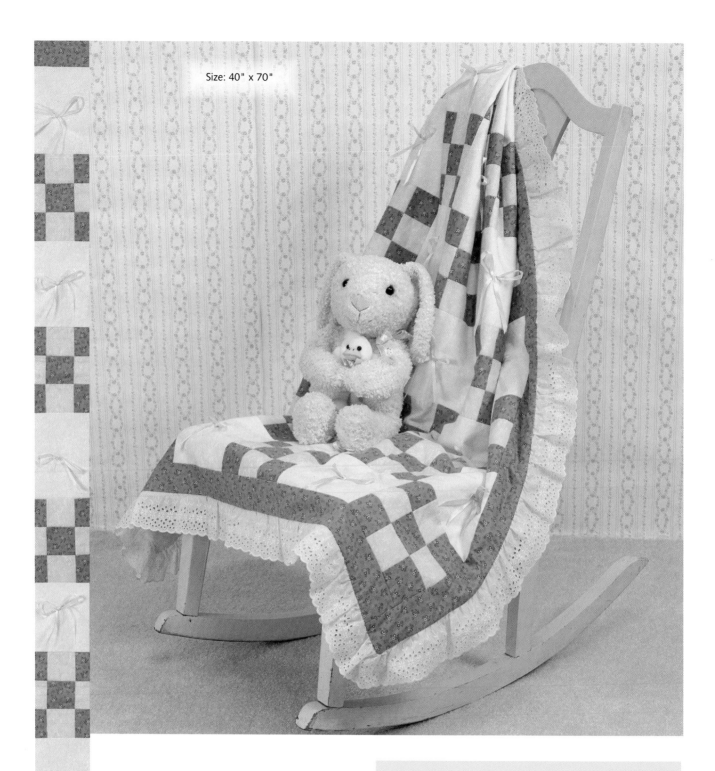

Size: 40" x 70"

Precious Patches Quilt

Another simple nine-patch that becomes an adorable baby quilt with the addition of coordinating bows.

Yardage

½ yd. light fabric for the nine-patches (peach)
⅔ yd. dark fabric for the nine-patches (green)
⅔ yd. for the solid squares
½ yd. for the borders
38" x 48" piece of fabric for the backing
38" x 48" piece of batting
5 yd. gathered eyelet
5 yd. ribbon for the bows

Nine-Patch Quilt Yardages

Quilt sizes are without borders. All strips are 42"/44".

Quilt Size	Strip Width	Strip Set Width*	Segments per Strip	Nine-Patch Block Size**	Yardage – Dark (green)	Yardage – Light (peach)	Yardage for 17 Solid Blocks
15" x 21"	1½"	3½"	28	3½" x 3½"	¼ yd.	5"	¼ yd.
22" x 31"	2"	5"	21	5" x 5"	⅓ yd.	¼ yd.	½ yd.
30" x 42"	2½"	6½"	16	6½" x 6½"	⅔ yd.	½ yd.	⅔ yd.
37" x 52"	3"	8"	14	8" x 8"	⅔ yd.	½ yd.	1 yd.
45" x 63"	3½"	9½"	12	9½" x 9½"	1 yd.	¾ yd.	1⅓ yd.

*If your strip set measures more or less, use your measurement to mark the ruler and cut the segments.

**If your block size measures more or less, use your measurement to cut strips for the solid blocks.

Make the nine-patch quilt blocks.

1. Cut seven light strips (2½" x 42").

2. Cut eight dark strips (2½" x 42").

3. Follow the directions for making nine-patch blocks on pages 43-44, marking the ruler at 2½" (the width of the above strips) to cut the segments.

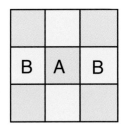

Cut the solid squares.

1. Mark the height (approximately 6½") of the nine-patch on a ruler using tape or a piece of static sticker. If your nine-patch measures more or less than 6½", use your measurement.

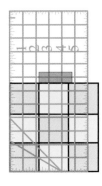

2. Cut three strips the same width as your nine-patch blocks (approximately 6½").

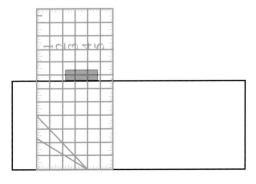

3. Cut these strips into squares.

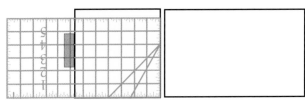

Accuracy Check

Fold the segment diagonally. The corners should line up perfectly.

If the corners do not line up, re-measure and re-mark the strip set width on the ruler.

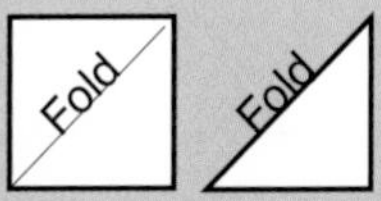

Sew the blocks into rows.

1. Sew the rows alternating the pieced and solid blocks, following the quilt diagram.

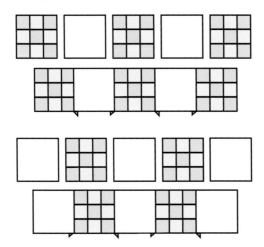

2. Set the seams. Press the seam allowances toward the solid colored squares. (See Chapter 1 for directions on setting seams and pressing for accuracy.)

Sew the rows together.

1. Match the seamlines. The seam allowances should be going in opposite directions at each seamline because each seam allowance was pressed toward the solid strip.

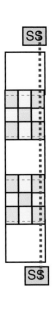

Some of the seams interlock. An interlocking seam is easy to match. The top seam allowance is toward the needle (away from you). The bottom seam allowance is toward you. Your sewing machine will help you match interlocking seams. As you sew, finger pin (hold the matching seamlines together). The machine pushes the top seam into the center of the bottom seam and locks it into place.

Some of the seams do not interlock. The top seam is toward you and the bottom seam is toward the machine. As you sew, finger pin (hold the matching seamlines together) or pin the seamlines together. (See page 30 for directions on pinning and finger pinning.)

2. Start sewing on a Starter Scrap (SS). Sew right sides together, matching the seamlines, and end with a Starter Scrap.

3. Set the seams. Press the seam allowances all in one direction.

Add the borders.

1. Cut six border strips (2-1/2" x 42"). See Emily's Quilt (pages 15-16) for information on cutting and sewing the border strips.

2. Keep your quilt square by making the quilt fit the border.

Add the eyelet.

1. Sew the eyelet to the quilt top, right sides together, with the gathered edge of the eyelet even with the outside of the quilt.

2. The corners need more gathering to lay nicely, so as you approach a corner, gather the eyelet more by pulling on the gathering thread in the eyelet. If the eyelet has a band on the raw edge, remove about 9" of the band and gather this section of eyelet by running a row of basting stitches.

3. Sew around the corner and continue stitching.

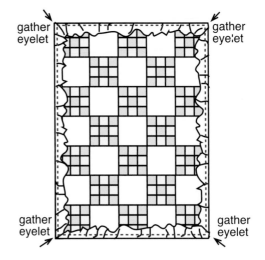

Finish the quilt.

1. Use an envelope-style finish. Refer to the A Step Above Quilt on page 34.

2. Quilt by tying with ribbons. Cut the ribbons into 12" lengths. Tie each into a bow. Cut the tails even.

3. Pin the bows to the quilt top. Use thread that matches the ribbon. Lower the feed dogs on the machine and bartack (zigzag) over the center of each bow.

Tip

If you are including the bows on this quilt, make sure that it is used as a wall quilt to ensure the baby's safety. If you are omitting the bows, quilt an appropriate design in the alternate blocks.

Size: 5" x 5"

This would be a good fat quarter project! Use one light and one dark fat quarter.

Uneven Nine-Patch Pot Holders

A nine-patch block is made from nine pieces, usually all identically sized squares. These blocks are called uneven because the center strip is cut wider than the top and bottom strips, thus the strips are uneven.

Two different blocks can be made: one with the narrow A segments on the outside and one with the narrow B segments on the outside. Make two different pot holders with plain backs or use one of the pot holders for the front and one for the back.

You can also create a simple quilt using all of one block or both blocks.

Yardage: 2 pot holders

7" x 9" piece of each fabric
8" x 8" square of batting*

*Insul-Bright™ batting by the Warm™ Company is made especially for potholders.

Uneven Nine-Patch Blocks
All strips are 42"/44".

Block Size	Narrow Strip Width	Wide Strip Width	Strip Set Width	Narrow Segments per Strip	Wide Segments per Strip
3½"	1¼"	2"	3½"	32	14
4½"	1½"	2½"	4½"	28	13
5½"	1¾"	3"	5½"	24	12
6½"	2"	3½"	6½"	21	10
7½"	2¼"	4½"	7½"	18	9
8½"	2½"	5"	8½"	16	8
9½"	2¾"	5½"	9½"	15	7
10½"	3"	6"	10½"	14	7

Sew the strip sets.

1. Cut two strips (1¾" x 9") from each fabric.

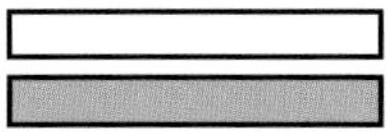

2. Cut one strip (3" x 9") from each fabric.

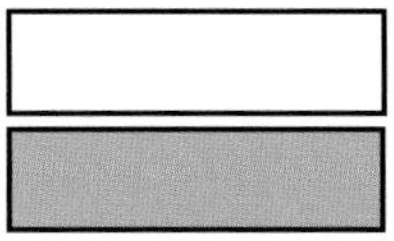

3. Sew three strips together as shown for each strip set.

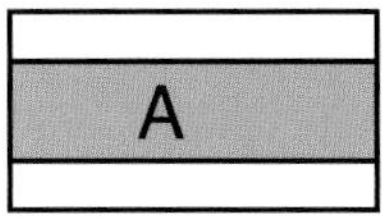

4. Set the seams. Press the seam allowances toward the darker fabric. (See Chapter 1 for directions on setting seams and pressing for accuracy.)

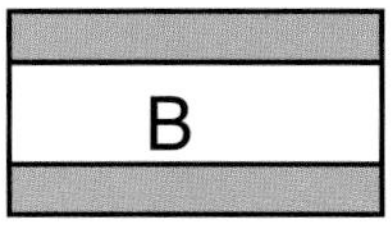

5. Straighten the strip sets, referring to page 9.

Decide on the blocks.
With these strip sets, two different blocks can be made.
This block has two narrow A segments and one wide B segment.

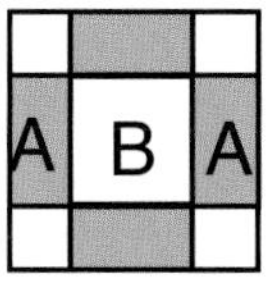

This block has two narrow B segments and one wide A segment.

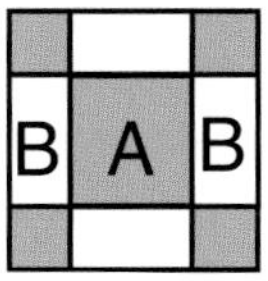

Cut the segments.

1. Mark a ruler at 1¾" (the width of the narrow strip) using tape or static sticker.

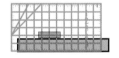

2. Use this mark on the ruler to cut the strip sets into the narrow segments needed.

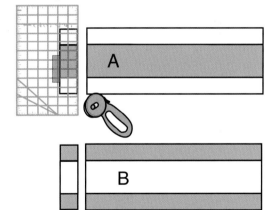

Accuracy Tip
Line up a cross line on the ruler with the seamline.

3. Mark a ruler at 3" (the width of the wide strip) on a ruler using tape or static sticker.

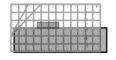

4. Use this mark on the ruler to cut the strip sets into the wide segments needed.

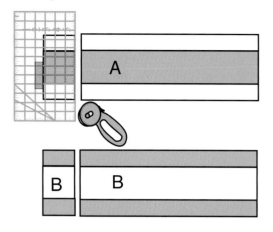

Sew the blocks.

Sew the segments into blocks, following the sewing directions for the nine-patch quilt block on pages 46.

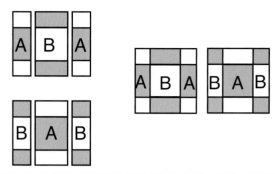

Accuracy Check

Fold the segment diagonally. The corners should line up perfectly.

If the corners do not line up, re-measure and re-mark the strip set width on the ruler.

Finish the potholders.

Add a hanging tab and use an envelope finish, referring to page 38.

Drug Stores Are Not Always Drug Stores

While teaching in The Hague in Holland, a friend of mine got sick, and we had to call the hotel doctor. He wrote a prescription, and another friend took a cab to the drug store.

NO, NO, NO! The drug store is where they sell drugs; prescriptions are filled at the pharmacy.

What Do They Think?

A sign posted outside a drug store in Amsterdam: "5397 miles to Wall Drug Store, South Dakota."

Wow! I bet they can't wait to see that drug store!

Since You're Not Busy!

One of my staff got sick while working at our booth at the International Quilt Festival in Houston. She was really dizzy and lost vision in one eye. The diagnosis from the doctor at the hospital was a migraine.

The paramedics arrived and were treating her. I was holding her hand, trying to calm her down, when a quilter reached around the paramedic and under my arm to ask if I would autograph her book since I wasn't doing anything.

Throw Mama From The Train

The European trains are great, but they don't allow much time to enter and exit. I had my crutches, wheelchair, and two suitcases. Finally, we had a system: My two friends would throw the wheelchair, crutches, and our suitcases out while I got myself out the door.

Four Hours To Go Five Blocks

While working at my booth at the International Quilt Festival in Houston, a shelf holding a quilt fell and hit me between the eyes. I was a little dizzy, but I had a class to teach so medical care could wait.

There were twice as many students in class as had registered, or could it be that I was seeing double?

My mind must have been on automatic because I don't remember anything I said during the class, but my assistant said she didn't know anything was wrong with me.

After class, the staff at the festival insisted I go to the hospital. That is where the comedy of errors begins.

We had to ride the bus back to the hotel to pick up the rental car. On the way to the hotel, the bus was in a minor accident. The staff member accompanying me was outside with the police when the bus driver left to go to the hotel.

I got off at the hotel and waited for the staff member in the lobby. After she arrived, she realized she didn't have the keys to the car. So we took a cab to the hospital.

Four hours after we left the convention center, the doctor treated me and wrote his report: slight concussion and nose broken by falling quilt. (Everybody's a comedian).

While leaving the hospital, I looked out a window, and what did I see? The convention center only four or five blocks away. We could have walked to the hospital.

Windowpane Crib Quilt

The Windowpane Crib Quilt is made up of continuous, uneven nine-patch blocks. The blocks are not separated with sashing strips or solid blocks.

The pieced part of this quilt is framed with an accent strip, which is a narrow folded strip that frames the pieced blocks. It is inserted between the blocks and the first border. The folded edge of the accent strip is loose and adds dimension to the quilt.

A coordinating five-pointed star pillow is on page 98.

Yardage

1 yd. dark fabric for blocks
1 yd. light fabric for blocks
⅞ yd. for accent strip and binding
¾ yd. for the borders
43" x 59" piece of coordinating fabric for the backing
43" x 59" piece of batting

Uneven Nine-Patch Yardages for 24 blocks (4 x 6)

Quilt sizes are without borders. All strips are 42"/44".

Quilt Size	Narrow Strip Width	Segments per Narrow Strip Set	Wide Strip Width	Segments per Wide Strip Set	Strip Set Width*	Block Size	Yardage**
16" x 24"	1½"	28	2½"	14	4½"	4½" x 4½"	¼ yd.
20" x 30"	1¾"	24	3"	12	5½"	5½" x 5½"	⅓ yd.
24" x 36"	2"	21	3½"	10	6½"	6½" x 6½"	½ yd.
28" x 42"	2¼"	18	4"	9	7½"	7½" x 7½"	⅔ yd.
32" x 48"	2½"	16	4½"	8	8½"	8½" x 8½"	⅔ yd.
36" x 54"	2¾"	15	5"	7	9½"	9½" x 9½"	1 yd.
40" x 60"	3"	14	5½"	7	10½"	10½" x 10½"	1 yd.

*If your strip set measures more or less, use your measurement to mark the ruler and cut the segments.

**This yardage is needed for each of the two fabrics.

Make the uneven nine-patch blocks.

1. Cut six strips (2¼" x 42"/44") from each of the nine-patch fabrics.

Cut three strips (4¼" x 42"/44") from each of the nine-patch fabrics.

2. Follow the instructions on page 53 to make 12 of each of the two variations of this block. Use the 2¼" and 4¼" measurements to mark a ruler and cut the segments.

 24 narrow A segments, 12 wide B segments

 12 wide A segments, 24 narrow B segments

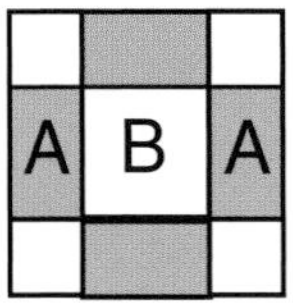

Sew the blocks into rows.

1. Sew four blocks together, matching seamlines, for each row.

2. Sew six identical rows.

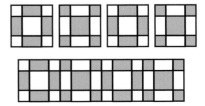

3. Set the seams. Press the seams all to the left in the first row; to the right in the second row, etc. (See Chapter 1 for directions on setting seams and pressing for accuracy.)

Sew the rows together.

1. Turn every other row upside down to create the design shown.

2. Sew the rows together, matching seamlines. The seam allowances should be going in opposite directions at each seamline because each seam allowance was pressed to the darker fabric. (See page 46 for more information on matching these seamlines.)

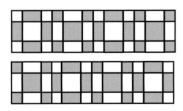

3. Set the seams. Press these seams all in one direction.

Make the accent strips.

1. Cut six (1½" x 42"/44") accent strips.

2. Sew two of these strips together for each of the side accent strips. (The directions for measuring and cutting the length of the accent strips are the same as for borders in Emily's Quilt, pages 15-16.)

3. Fold and press the strips in half lengthwise, wrong sides together, using this QuickFold technique:

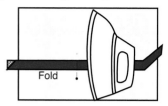

a. Fold one end of the strip.
b. Put a pin in the ironing pad and up over the strip and into the pad.
c. Pull the folded strip under the pin and under the iron.

Sew accent strips.

The accent strip will lay loose on the quilt top with the fold toward the quilt.

1. Pin the accent strips on the right side of the quilt even with the top and bottom edges. Use as many pins as necessary.

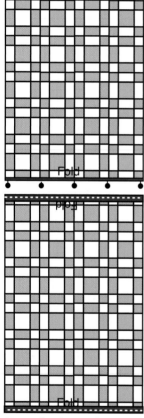

2. Sew with the accent strip on top. Remove the pins as you come to them; do not sew over the pins.

3. Do NOT press the seam allowances.

New stitching lines are shown in white.

4. Pin and sew the side accent strips even with the sides of the quilt top; the fold will lay toward the quilt. The fold will lay loose on the quilt top.

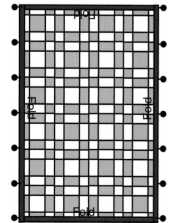

5. Sew with the accent strip on top. Remove the pins as you come to them; do not sew over the pins.

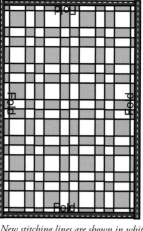

New stitching lines are shown in white.

6. Do NOT press the seam allowances.

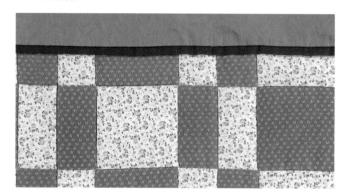

Borders

1. Cut two strips (4" x width of the quilt top) for the top and bottom borders. Measure the length needed (see page 15).

2. Pin a border strip to the raw edge of the accent strip at the quilt top and bottom.

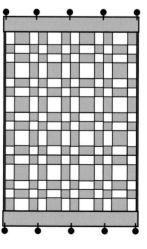

3. Sew with the border strip on top. Remove the pins as you come to them; do not sew over the pins.

4. Set the stitches. Press the seam allowances toward the border strip.

New stitching lines are shown in red.

5. Cut four strips (4" x 42"/44") for the side borders.

6. Sew two of these strips together to make the strip long enough for the side borders. Cut the strip to the exact length of the quilt.

7. Pin the border strip to the raw edge of the accent strip and the quilt top, matching the center seam to the center of the quilt top.

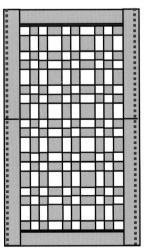

New stitching lines are shown in red.

8. Sew with the border strip on top. Remove the pins as you come to them; do not sew over the pins.

9. Set the stitches. Press the seam allowances toward the border strip.

Finish the quilt.

1. Layer the quilt top, batting, and backing, following the directions on page 137.

2. Cut five strips (3" x 42"/44") for the binding. This is enough for a ½" finished binding, which will coordinate well with the ½" width of the accent strip.

3. Follow the directions on pages 139-142 for binding the quilt.

Quilt made by Lori Jonsson
Size: 32" x 42" (5 blocks x 7 blocks)

Squares Galore Quilt

This uneven nine-patch quilt uses sashing strips to frame each individual block.

Yardage

1 yd. dark fabric for the nine-patches
⅔ yd. light fabric for the nine-patches
⅛ yd. dark fabric for the sashing
½ yd. light fabric for the sashing
½ yd. for the borders
43" x 59" piece of fabric for the backing
43" x 59" piece of batting
½ yd. for the binding

Make the uneven nine-patch blocks.

1. Cut six strips (1½" x 42") from each of the nine-patch fabrics.

2. Cut three strips (3" x 42") from each of the nine-patch fabrics.

3. Make 35 blocks, following the instructions on pages 53-54.

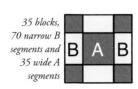

35 blocks, 70 narrow B segments and 35 wide A segments

Cut the sashing strips and squares.

1. Mark a ruler at 5" (the height of the quilt block) using tape or static sticker.
If your block measures more or less than 5", use your measurement.

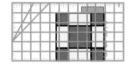

2. Cut 11 strips (1½" x 42") from the light sashing fabric.

3. Use the mark on the ruler to cut the sashing strips into segments needed.

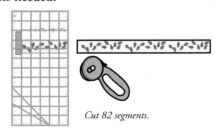

Cut 82 segments.

4. Cut two strips (1½" x 42") from the dark sashing fabric.

5. Cut these strips into the squares needed.

Cut 48 1½" squares.

Sew into rows.

1. Sew the sashing strips and blocks into five identical rows.

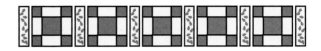

2. Keep your quilt square. Make the quilt block fit the sashing strip. Line up the tops of the block and the sashing strip.

3. Start with a Starter Scrap (SS). See Chapter 1. Sew with the sashing strip on top. Sew a few stitches. STOP.

4. Hold the bottoms together so they match, then sew to the end.

5. Chainstitch from one piece to the next, ending with a Starter Scrap.

6. Set the seams. Press the seam allowances toward the sashing strip. (See Chapter 1 for directions on setting seams and pressing for accuracy.)

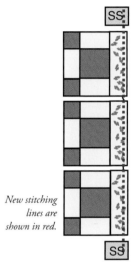

New stitching lines are shown in red.

Sew the pieced sashing strips.

1. Sew together six dark sashing squares and five light sashing strips into eight long sashing strips.

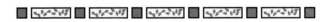

2. Set the seams. Press the seam allowances toward the sashing strips and away from the squares.

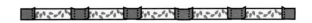

Sew the rows together.

1. Line up the seamlines on the pieced sashing strip with the seamlines in the row. The seamlines will lay in opposite directions, which will help to match the seamlines. Some seamlines will interlock and some will not, see the Rail Fence Quilt on page 30 for more information.

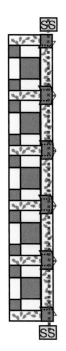

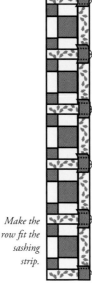

Make the row fit the sashing strip.

2. Sew with the sashing strip on top.

3. Set the seams. Press the seam allowances toward the sashing strip.

Sew the borders.

1. Cut four border strips (3" x 42").

2. Sew the side borders first for this quilt. If they are sewn on after the top and bottom borders, each side will need to be pieced. (For instructions on measuring, cutting, and sewing borders, see Emily's Quilt on pages 15-16.)

Finish the quilt.

Directions for layering, quilting, and binding quilts can be found in Chapter 8.

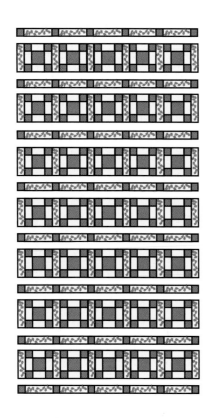

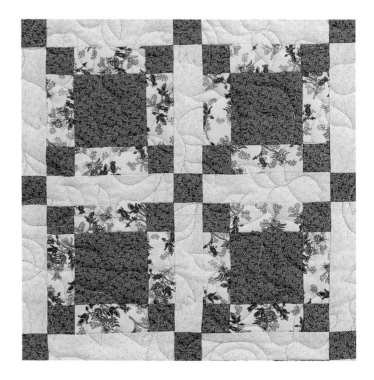

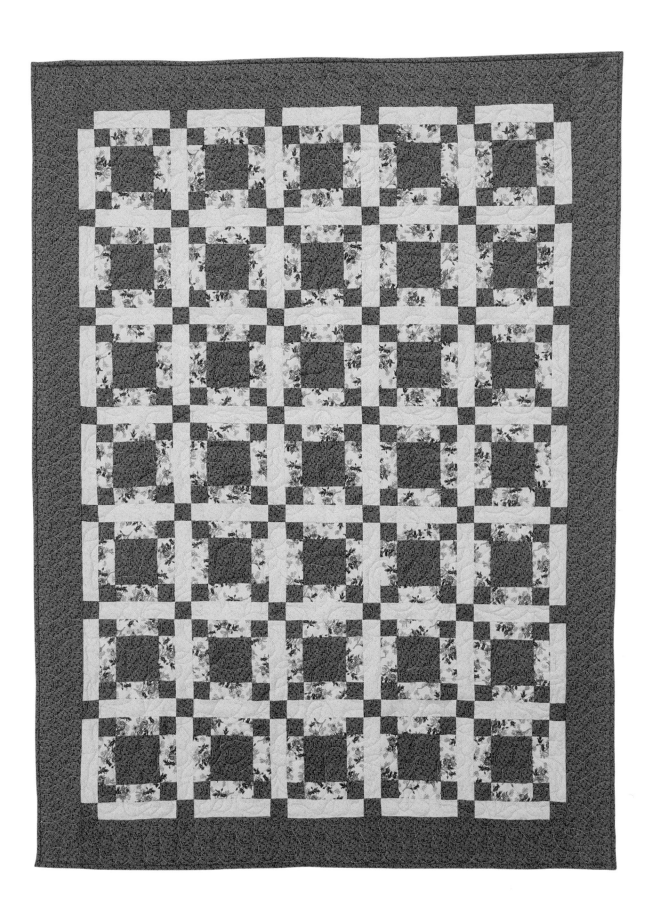

Chapter 5

From Strips to Stars

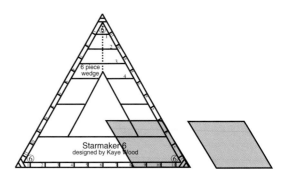

Have you heard any of the following pieces of advice?

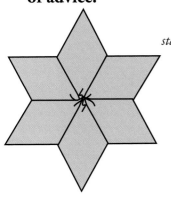

"The tent in the middle of the star will quilt out."
No it won't!

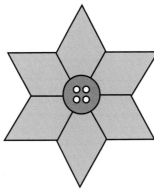

"A star needs to have a button in the middle because the points don't quite match."
No, it doesn't!

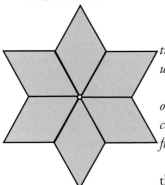

"You have to take one or two stitches by hand to close up the hole in the center."
Or, *"You have to rip out one or two stitches in the center of the star so it will lay flat."*
We've all heard these things!

Stars become easier and the centers lay flat when the angles are accurate and the seams are anchored.

The Starmaker Master Templates ensure the accuracy, and my technique of anchoring eliminates the problems with the center of the star.

The Starmakers can be used to cut many different shapes, only some of which are shown in this book.

How can you strip cut diamonds for stars?

It is possible to cut patterns you already have with the Starmaker Master Templates.

Take a look at the diamond template given with the pattern you want to make.

Lay one of the Starmakers on your template. Don't worry about the size. If the angle is the same as any one

of the angles on the Starmakers, that angle can be used to strip cut the diamond.

You need to know two things:
• the size of the template and
• the angle of the diamond

<u>Size:</u>
The size of the diamond is determined by the width of the strip. To measure the size (height) of the diamond, imagine it lying on a strip and measure the height.

This is the strip width needed to cut this size diamond. The top and bottom edges of the strip become the top and bottom of the diamond.

<u>Angle:</u>
The angle is cut with one of the Starmaker Master Templates.

How the Strip Cut Stars developed

In 1976, I realized that I could progress from stripping simple squares into star designs by just changing the angle.

All of us who do strip piecing should thank Barbara Johannah for starting the stripping revolution. Her book, "The Quick Quiltmaking Handbook," published in 1979, made my creative juices start flowing.

After studying a lot of quilt designs, I noticed that the same angles were repeated. The pieces might range from miniature to large, but the angle remained the same.

What would happen if I expanded on Barbara's idea of stripping with a way to cut accurate angles regardless of size?

Thus, the Starmaker® Master Template concept was born. I thought they would only make stars, so I called them Starmakers. By placing the Starmaker on a strip, I could cut diamonds, which, when sewn together, would make stars. The size of the diamond would depend on the width of the strip, so any size diamond could be made.

This was in 1981. The first Starmakers were made from a thin plastic, because this was BRC (Before Rotary Cutters).

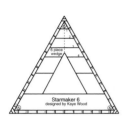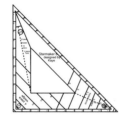

After two years, I changed the Starmakers to a thicker plastic because rotary cutters were now available. I also added more lines to make them more versatile.

In 1982, my first book, "Quilt Like A Pro," was published. This introduced some basic designs using the Starmakers. Everything I knew about quilting at that time is included in "Quilt Like A Pro."

Since 1981, the Starmakers have gotten much smarter and more versatile as I learned how to use them to cut more than 140 different shapes in my quilts; these cutting techniques are included in my book, "Starmaker Design Concepts."

Think about the angles in the quilt patterns you have made. Maybe some of them can be made using just one of the three Starmaker Master Templates.

With the three Starmakers, cut these angles:
Starmaker 8: 90°, 45°, 22.5°.
Starmaker 6: 60°, 30°
Starmaker 5: 90°, 72°, 18°, 9°

But forget the math. My techniques are easy to follow, and you won't even be aware of the mathematical principles I've used. If math is your thing, you will know why my techniques work so well.

The Starmaker Master Templates are used in over 25 of my quilting books and several books by other authors. They have made my quilting life so much easier.

Easier, faster, more accurate. What more could you ask for?

Eating in restaurants

You Wouldn't Like What You Ordered

Has this ever happened to you?

Four of us ordered our food, and we all ordered something different. When our dinner arrived, I had the same thing as one of the other people.

"Is this what I ordered?"

The waiter said, "You wouldn't have liked what you ordered."

Chicken In A Bowl

What would you think that was? I thought it would be like chicken pot pie, so I ordered it.

Wrong!

The waitress asked, "Are you sure that's what you want? It's a chicken in a bowl."

And that is what it was. A whole chicken sitting in a bowl of clear broth.

If I had had the same waiter as above, he would have said nothing, just brought me something else to eat.

Quilt made by Joyce Horn, Lori Jonsson and Kathleen Quinlan

Size: 41" x 60"

Star-Spangled Sampler Quilt

Appliquéd stars in red, white, and blue add a patriotic accent to any décor.

Yardage

½ yd. dark fabric for stars
½ yd. light fabric for stars
1 yd. interfacing for stars*
1¼ yd. red for background squares
1 yd. blue for square borders
1 yd. for sashing/border strips
45" x 65" piece of fabric for backing
45" x 65" piece of batting
⅓ yd. for binding

Use a lightweight interfacing or pattern tracing fabric to face the stars.

Each of the six stars is strip cut from the same width strip set.

The sizes of the stars in this quilt are different only because of the sharpness of the angles of the star points. The five-pointed star is the smallest; the eight-pointed star is the largest. Because the stars are different sizes, different width borders are added to the star squares to make the blocks finish the same size.

These stars have finished edges. They are faced (lightweight interfacing sewn right sides together to the star), turned right-side out, and machine appliquéd to the background squares.

Each pinwheel star could also be made into a matching pillow.

Different star finishes are included in Chapter 7.

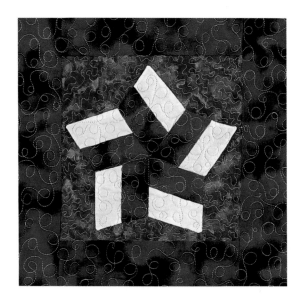

Five-Pointed Pinwheel Stars: Cutting Techniques

Make the strip sets.

1. Cut one strip (2" x 42") from each of the star fabrics. (See Chapter 1 for accurate cutting directions.)

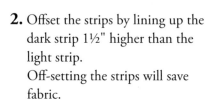

Strip widths for different size stars are shown in the chart.

2. Offset the strips by lining up the dark strip 1½" higher than the light strip.
Off-setting the strips will save fabric.

3. Sew two strips together into a strip set, using ¼" seam allowances.

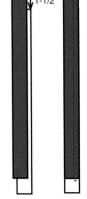

New stitching lines are shown in white.

4. Set the seams. Press the seam allowances toward the darker fabric. (See Chapter 1 for setting seams and pressing accurately.)

Cut the strip set at an angle.

1. Mark the width of the strip set (approximately 3½") on a ruler using tape or a piece of static sticker.

Accuracy Tip:
This is the measurement used to cut the strip set into segments.

2. Place the bottom of the Starmaker 5 along the bottom of the strip. The 5 in a circle on the Starmaker 5 is at the bottom right-hand side of the strip.

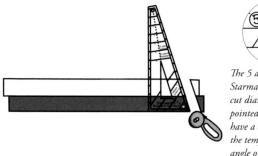

The 5 angle of the Starmaker 5 is used to cut diamonds for five-pointed stars. If you don't have a Starmaker 5, use the template for the 5 angle on page 70.

3. Cut the strip along the right-hand side of the Starmaker 5.

Cut the diamond segments.

1. Place the ruler on the strip so the mark on the ruler lines up with the cut end of the strip.

2. Butt the Starmaker 5 up against the ruler. Make sure the bottom of the Starmaker 5 lines up with the bottom of the strip.

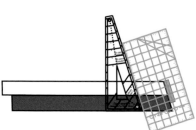

3. Remove the ruler and cut along the right-hand side of the Starmaker 5.

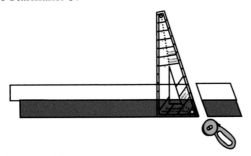

Accuracy Check:

Fold the segment diagonally. The corners should line up perfectly.

If the corners do not line up, re-measure and re-mark the strip set width on the ruler.

4. Cut 10 diamonds (five for each star) using the ruler for size and the Starmaker 5 for accurate angles. **Note:** Using just the ruler without the Starmaker 5 will not ensure accurate angles.

Out Of Gas

Do you know that in Michigan the state police carry extra gas in their patrol cars?

On my way to Paducah, I ran out of gas. Soon a state trooper stopped. He stayed in his car longer than I thought was necessary—probably doing a check on my license plate.

Getting out of the car, his hand was adjusting his gun and club, getting ready to protect himself.

As he approached, I raised my hands and said, "Don't even ask if my gas gauge works."

"That's a question only a husband would ask," he said as he began putting gas into my tank.

I couldn't resist asking him if the police in every state carry extra gas.

"Why?" he asked.

"Well, if you had lots of time and wanted to go cross country without buying gas, could you do it?"

"I'm writing your name down just in case."

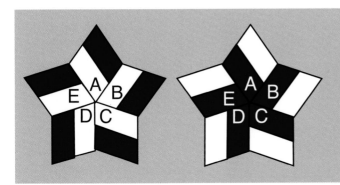

Accurate sewing of the five-pointed stars is accomplished by anchoring two sets of points.

This means points A and B are anchored (sewn together all the way from edge to edge); points C and D are also anchored. When the E point is inserted, the center of the star will lay flat.

Five-Pointed Pinwheel Stars

All strips are 42"/44" long.

Strip Width	Strip Set Width	Diamonds per Strip Set	Height of Star
1½"	2½"	16	8"
2"	3½"	11	10"
2½"	4½"	8	13"
3"	5½"	7	16½"
3½"	6½"	6	19½"

Five-Pointed Stars Using the Starmaker 5 Master Template

If you don't have a Starmaker 5, use the 5 angle at right to mark and cut diamonds.

The 5 in a circle on the Starmaker 5 means five pieces cut with this angle will make a five-pointed star.

Five-Pointed Stars:
Place the bottom of the Starmaker 5 on the bottom of the strip of fabric. Cut the strip along the angle at the right-hand side of the Starmaker 5. Follow the directions on the following pages for cutting diamonds.

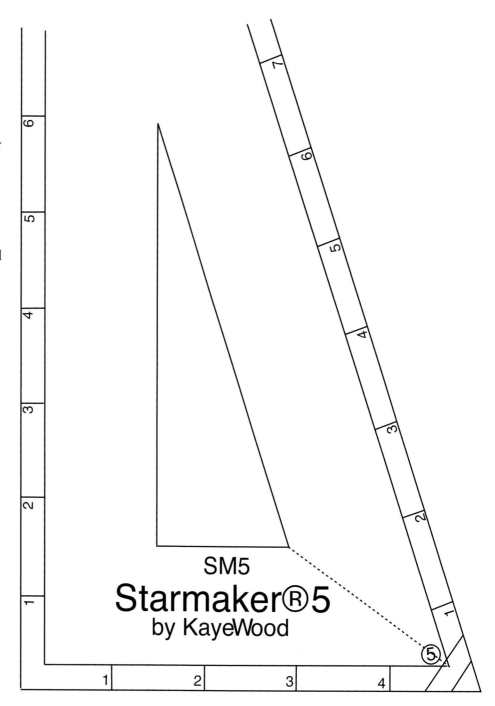

SM5
Starmaker®5
by KayeWood

Five-Pointed Pinwheel Star: Sewing Techniques

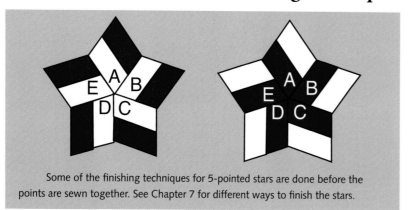

Some of the finishing techniques for 5-pointed stars are done before the points are sewn together. See Chapter 7 for different ways to finish the stars.

Make the diamonds.
Cut five diamonds for each pinwheel star. Refer to the directions on pages 68-69.

Sew the diamonds into sets.

Follow the diagrams for either the light- or the dark-centered stars.

1. Line up all sides of the A diamond on top of the B diamond, and the C diamond on top of the D diamond.

Light centers: The light strip is at the top of the A and C diamonds and to the right-hand side of the B and D diamond.

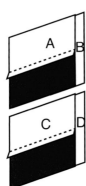

Dark centers: The dark strip is at the top of the A and C diamonds and at the right-hand side of the B and D diamonds.

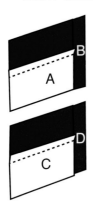

2. Start sewing on a Starter Scrap (see Chapter 1). Anchor this seam by sewing the A and B points, right sides together, all the way from one edge to the other edge.

3. Chainstitch to the C and D points, right sides together. Anchor this seam by sewing all the way from one edge to the other edge. Sew off onto a Starter Scrap (SS).

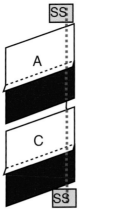
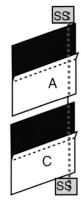

New stitching lines are shown in red.

4. Set the seams. Press the seam allowances toward the B and D diamonds. (See Chapter 1 for information on setting seams and pressing for accuracy.)

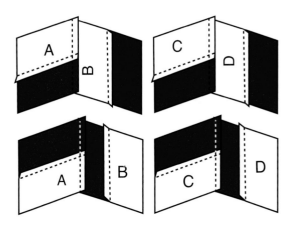

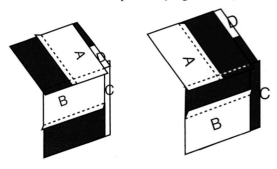

Add the E point.

1. Line up the center seams of the AB and CD points, right sides together. The seams will lay in opposite directions with the top seam lying toward you.

2. Before stitching, hold the seamlines together and lift the top seam allowance up so you can see the seamline between the A and B diamonds. Lifting the seam allowance is done to avoid sewing over any seamline.

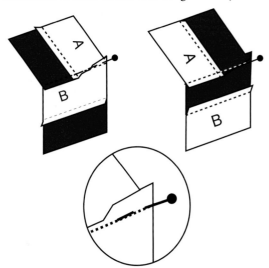

3. Place a pin directly through both seamlines. The pin serves two purposes: holding the seamlines together and increasing visibility. The shiny pin will make the seamline easier to see, because you need to start stitching right at the exact seamline.

Sew the diamond sets together.

The seam between the two sets of diamonds is not anchored, which means you will not sew over any seamlines.

1. Start sewing on the pinned seamline between the A and B points. Lock stitch by taking three or four stitches on this seamline.

2. Sew to the outside edges.

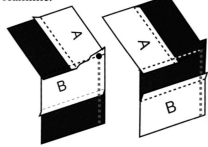

3. Set the seams. Press the seam allowances away from the B diamond and toward the C diamond.

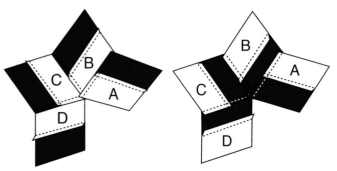

Add the E point.

1. Line up the E point underneath, right sides up; with the D point on top, right sides down. All edges of these two diamonds should line up.

2. While holding the seamlines together, pull the seam allowance back so you can see the seamline between the C and D diamonds.

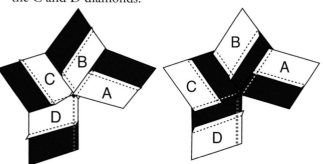

3. Start sewing on this seamline. Lock stitch by taking three or four stitches on the seamline.

4. Sew to the outside edges.

5. Set the seams. Press the seam allowances toward the E diamond.

Sew the seam between E and A points.

1. Line up the edges of the E and A diamonds.

2. While holding the seamlines together, lift the seam allowances up so you can see the seamline between the D and E diamonds.

3. Start sewing on this seamline. Lockstitch by taking three or four stitches on the seamline.

4. Sew to the outside edges.

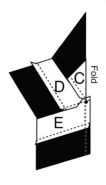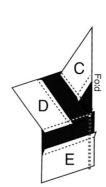

5. Set the seams. Press the seam allowances toward the A diamond.

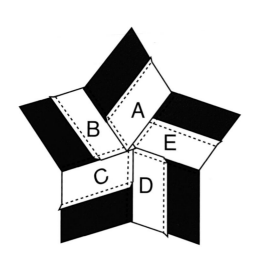

Six-Pointed Pinwheel Stars: Cutting Techniques

Make the strip sets.

1. Cut two strips (2" x 42") from each of the star fabrics. (See Chapter 1 for accurate cutting directions.)

Strip widths for different size stars are shown in the chart.

2. Offset the strips by lining up the dark strip 2" higher than the light strip. Offsetting the strips will save fabric.

3. Sew two strips together into a strip set, using ¼" seam allowances.

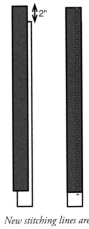

New stitching lines are shown in white.

4. Set the seams. Press the seam allowances toward the darker fabric. (See Chapter 1 for directions on setting seams and pressing for accuracy.)

Cut the strip set at an angle.

1. Mark the width of the strip set (approximately 3½") on a ruler using tape or a piece of static sticker.

Accuracy Tip:
This is the measurement used to cut the strip set into segments.

2. Place the bottom of the Starmaker 6 along the bottom of the strip. The 6 in a circle on the Starmaker 6 is at the bottom right-hand side of the strip.

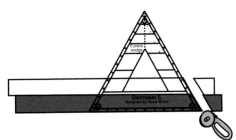

The 6 angle of the Starmaker 6 is used to cut diamonds for a 6-pointed star. If you don't have a Starmaker 6, use the template for the 6 angle of the Starmaker 6 on page 75.

3. Cut the strip along the right-hand side of the Starmaker 6.

Cut the diamond segments.

1. Place the ruler on the strip so the mark on the ruler lines up with the cut end of the strip.

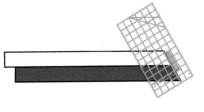

2. Butt the Starmaker 6 up against the ruler. Make sure the bottom of the Starmaker 6 lines up with the bottom of the strip.

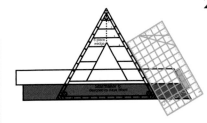

What Did She Say?

Did you ever teach a class to non-English-speaking students? How did I know they didn't speak English?

They didn't laugh at my jokes. What other reason could there be?

In Germany, I taught a Starmaker class to Japanese students. They understood the concepts and techniques and did very well in class, but they just didn't get the jokes.

Helen Can Do it!

During a consumer show, the vendor in the next booth was doing a demonstration. A gentleman watched for quite a while, then asked, "Do you really need to know anything to be able to do this?"

Unsure of how to answer, she said, "Not really. It is pretty easy."

"Good. I'll be back in a minute." He hurried down the aisle, yelling, "Helen, I found something you can do."

3. Remove the ruler and cut along the right-hand side of the Starmaker 6.

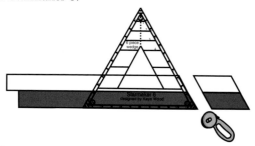

Accuracy Check:

Fold the segment diagonally. The corners should line up perfectly.

If the corners do not line up, re-measure and re-mark the strip set width on the ruler.

4. Cut 12 diamonds (6 for each star) using the ruler for size and the Starmaker 6 for accurate angles. **Note:** Using just the ruler without the Starmaker will not ensure accurate angles.

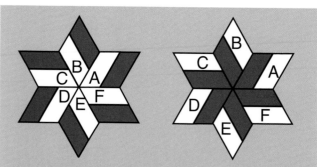

Accurate sewing of the six-pointed stars is accomplished by anchoring all of the points.

This means the points are sewn together all the way from edge-to-edge. The center seam is pressed open to reduce bulk.

Six-Pointed Pinwheel Stars

All strips are 42"/44" long.

Strip Width	Strip Set Width	Diamonds per Strip Set	Height of Star
1½"	2½"	13	9½"
2"	3½"	10	13"
2½"	4½"	7	17"
3"	5½"	6	21"
3½"	6½"	5	24"

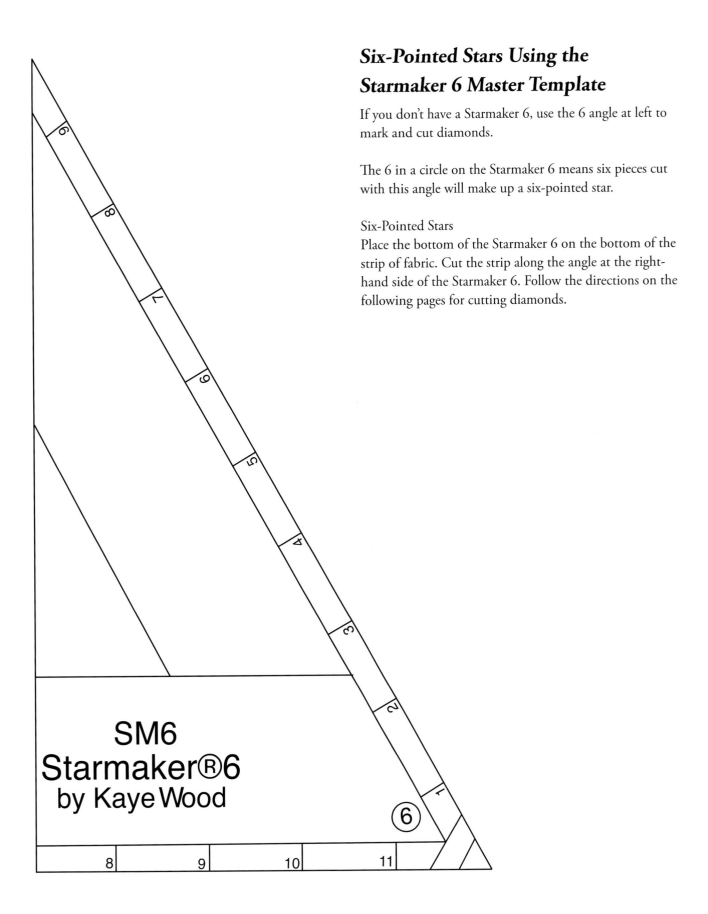

Six-Pointed Stars Using the Starmaker 6 Master Template

If you don't have a Starmaker 6, use the 6 angle at left to mark and cut diamonds.

The 6 in a circle on the Starmaker 6 means six pieces cut with this angle will make up a six-pointed star.

Six-Pointed Stars
Place the bottom of the Starmaker 6 on the bottom of the strip of fabric. Cut the strip along the angle at the right-hand side of the Starmaker 6. Follow the directions on the following pages for cutting diamonds.

Six-Pointed Pinwheel Star:

Sewing Techniques

Make the diamonds.

Cut six diamonds for each pinwheel star. Refer to the directions on pages 73-74.

Sew the diamonds into sets.

Follow the diagrams for either the light- or the dark-centered stars.

1. Line up all sides of the B diamond on top of the A diamond and the E diamond on top of the D diamond.

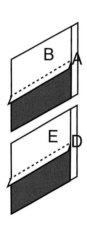

Light centers: The light strip is at the top of the B and E diamonds and to the right-hand side of the A and D diamonds.

Dark centers: The dark strip is at the top of the B and E diamonds and to the right side of the A and D diamonds.

2. Start sewing on a Starter Scrap (see Chapter 1). Anchor this seam by sewing the B and A points, right sides together, all the way from one edge to the other edge.

3. Chainstitch to the E and D points, right sides together. Anchor this seam by sewing all the way from one edge to the other edge. Sew off onto a Starter Scrap.

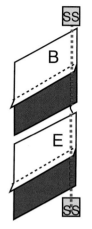 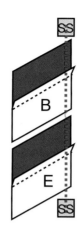

New stitching lines are shown in red.

4. Set the seams. Press both seam allowances away from the A and E diamond. (See Chapter 1 for information on setting seams and pressing for accuracy.)

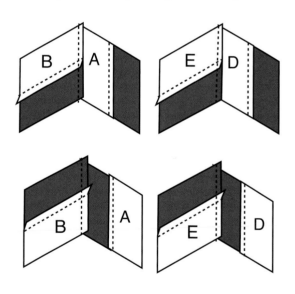

Add the third diamond to each set.

*A **Needle Match** is used for the V that forms at the top and bottom of the diamonds. At the top and bottom, the two segments overlap. The stitching line starts and stops at the point they overlap. Your sewing machine needle is used to line up the diamonds.*

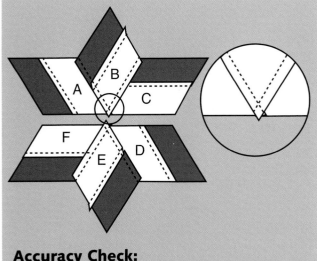

1. Put the sewing machine needle down into the machine. Insert the two segments under the machine presser foot, with the needle set to sew a ¼" seam. The needle will be in the exact spot where the two segments overlap.

   If the needle is not in the spot where the two segments overlap, leave the needle down and adjust the segments so they do overlap exactly at the needle.

2. Start sewing on a Starter Scrap and chainstitch to the next set of diamonds. Sew the C diamond to the B diamond. Sew the F diamond to the E diamond. Sew all the way from top to bottom to anchor this seam. Anchoring the seam at the outside of the star makes it easier to do the "Y" seams that are used to piece diamonds around the star; see page 96.

3. Set the seams. Press the seam allowances away from the middle (B and E) diamonds.

Accuracy Check:

The seamlines should cross ¼" from the outside edge. This allows for the seam allowance when the two half-stars are sewn together.

- If your seams cross at less than ¼" from the outside edge, your seam allowances between the points were sewn at less than ¼". Go back and take a little wider seam allowance.
- If your seams cross at more than ¼", your seam allowances between the points were sewn at more than ¼".

Sorry! It's time for a frog stitch (RIP-IT, RIP-IT, RIP-IT).

4. Trim the points of the seam allowances that extend past the half stars.

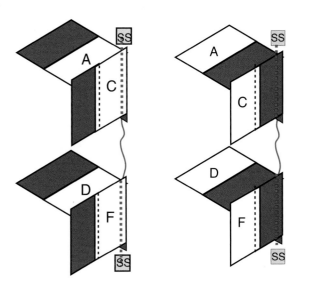

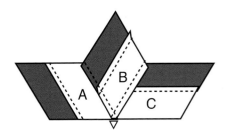

Match the two half-stars together.

Center Match with seamlines pressed away from middle diamond.

1. With right sides together, put a pin into the point (¼" from the edge) of one star half and through to the point on the right side of the other half.

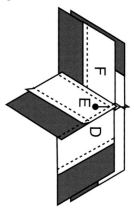

2. Do **not** turn the pin now. Hold the pin straight up and down through both points.

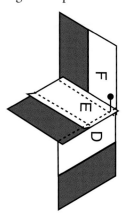

3. Hold the fabric in place between your thumb and finger; then turn the pin and bring the point of the pin up through the seamline. (For more accurate pinning, pin along the grain line of the fabric, which is usually along the seamline.)

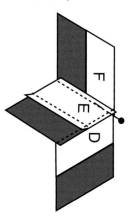

4. Put a second pin in along the other seamline, still holding the center together.

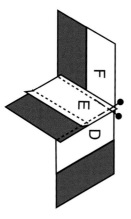

Sew the two half-stars together.

1. Set your machine for a basting stitch (a long stitch).

> If your points don't match on the first try, this basting stitch will be easier to rip out.
>
> If your points do match, great! Set your machine for a regular stitch and resew over the same line.

2. Starting with a Starter Scrap, sew the two pieces together.

3. When you get a few stitches from the center point, remove the first pin. At the center point, the seamline must go through the exact point where the seamlines cross. *If the point is slightly more or less than your seam allowance, sew directly over the point even if the point is slightly more or less than ¼".*

4. Remove the second pin and continue sewing.

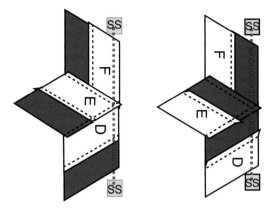

5. Set the center seamline and press the center seam open.

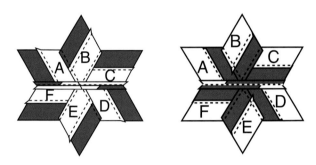

Matching Seams

In spite of all the accurate cutting, sewing, and pressing, some fabrics do not want to play together and match in the center. So I have some desperation matching techniques in Chapter 1. Try some of them when you are desperate.

Eight-Pointed Pinwheel Stars: Cutting Techniques

Make the strip sets.

1. Cut three strips (2") from each of the star fabrics. (See Chapter 1 for accurate cutting directions.)

Strip widths for different size stars are shown in the chart on the following page.

2. Offset the strips with the dark strip 2½" higher than the light strip. Offsetting the strips will save fabric.

3. Sew two strips together into a strip set, using ¼" seam allowances.

4. Set the seams. Press the seam allowances toward the darker fabric. (See Chapter 1 for directions on setting seams and pressing for accuracy.)

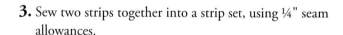

2-1/2"

New stitching lines are shown in red.

Cut the strip set at an angle.

1. Mark the width of the strip set (approximately 3½") on a ruler using tape or a piece of static sticker.

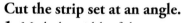

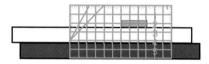

Accuracy Tip:
This is the measurement used to cut the strip set into segments.

2. Place the bottom of the Starmaker 8 along the bottom of the strip set.

3. Cut the strip along the right-hand side of the Starmaker 8.

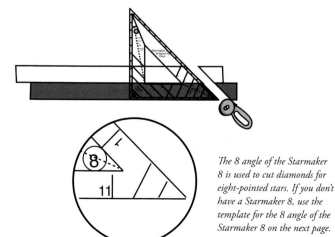

The 8 angle of the Starmaker 8 is used to cut diamonds for eight-pointed stars. If you don't have a Starmaker 8, use the template for the 8 angle of the Starmaker 8 on the next page.

Cut the diamond segments.

1. Place the ruler on the strip so the mark on the ruler lines up with the cut end of the strip set.

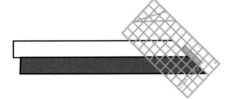

2. Butt the Starmaker 8 up against the ruler. Make sure the bottom of the Starmaker 8 lines up with the bottom of the strip.

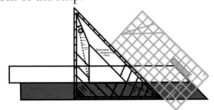

3. Remove the ruler and cut along the right-hand side of the Starmaker 8.

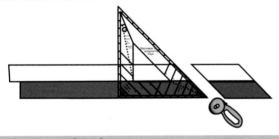

Accuracy Check:

Fold the segment diagonally. The corners should line up perfectly.

If the corners do not line up, re-measure and re-mark the strip set width on the ruler.

4. Cut 16 diamonds (eight for each star) using the ruler for distance and the Starmaker 8 for accurate angles.
Note: Using just the ruler without the Starmaker will not ensure accurate angles.

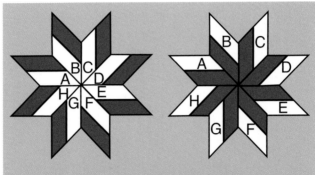

Accurate sewing of the eight-pointed star is accomplished by the anchoring of all the points.

All of the points are sewn together into groups of two. Two groups are then sewn together into a half star and joined together by matching the center seams.

The center seam is pressed open to reduce bulk.

Eight-Pointed Pinwheel Stars

All strips are 42"/44" long.

Strip Width	Strip Set Width	Diamonds per Strip Set	Height of Star
1½"	2½"	11	11"
2"	3½"	7	16"
2½"	4½"	5	20"

Eight-Pointed Stars Using the Starmaker 8 Master Template

If you don't have a Starmaker 8, use the template below for the 8 angle.

The 8 in a circle on the Starmaker 8 means eight pieces cut with this angle will make up an eight-pointed star.

Eight-Pointed Stars: Place the bottom of the Starmaker 8 on the bottom of the strip of fabric. Cut the strip along the angle at the right-hand side of the Starmaker 8.

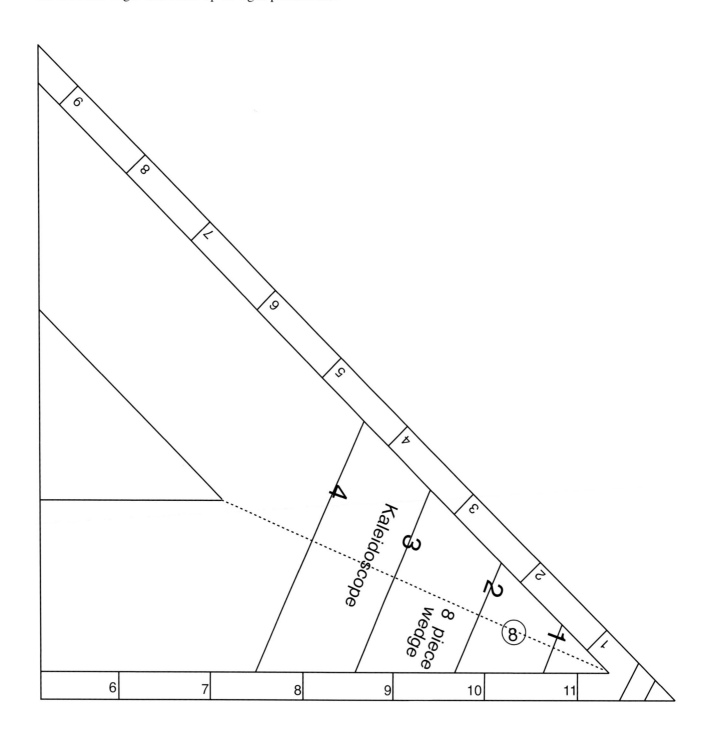

Eight-Pointed Pinwheel Stars: Sewing Techniques

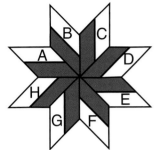

Make the diamonds.

1. Cut eight diamonds for each star. Refer to the directions on pages 80-81.

Sew the diamonds into sets.

Follow the diagrams for either the light- or the dark-centered stars.

1. Line up the diamonds in sets of two, matching up all four sides of the diamonds in each set. Line up: the A, C, E, and G diamonds on top of the B, D, F, and H diamonds.

> **Light centers:** The light strip is at the top of the A, C, E, and G diamonds. The light strip is to the right-hand side of the B, D, F, and H diamonds.

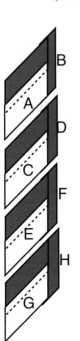

> **Dark centers:** The dark strip is at the top of the A, C, E, and G diamonds. The dark strip is to the right-hand side of the B, D, F, and H diamonds.

2. Start sewing on a Starter Scrap. Anchor the seams by sewing all the way from one edge to the next.

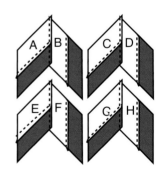

3. Chainstitch to the next sets of diamonds. Sew off to a Starter Scrap.

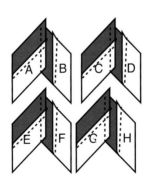

New stitching lines are shown in red.

4. Set the seams. Press both seam allowances toward the B, D, F, and H diamonds. (See Chapter 1 for information on setting stitches and pressing for accuracy.)

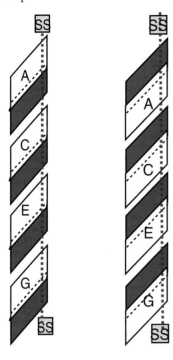

Sew two sets together.

1. Line up the top and right-hand side of the diamonds to be sewn:

> Line up the A and B diamond set with the C and D diamond set, right sides together.
>
> Line up the E and F diamond set with the G and H diamond set, right sides together.

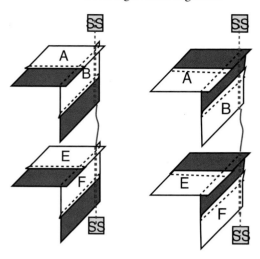

2. Place a pin diagonally through the matching seamlines. A needle match is used for the V that forms at the top of the diamonds. (See page 77 in this chapter for more information.)

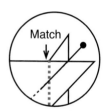

3. Start sewing on a Starter Scrap and chainstitch both sets of diamonds. Sew all the way from top to bottom to anchor the seamline at the outside of the star.

4. Trim the points from the seam allowance diagonally to reduce bulk.

5. Set the stitches. Press the seam allowances toward the C and G diamonds. Notice how the seam allowances go all to the left on the top half of the star and all to the right on the bottom half.

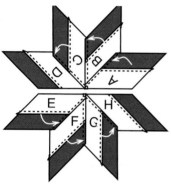

Accuracy Check:

   The seamlines should cross ¼" from the outside edge. This allows for the seam allowance when the two half-stars are sewn together.

- If your seamlines do not meet to form a point, ¼" from the edge, it's time for a frog stitch (rip-it, rip-it, rip-it). Rip out the stitches, re-pin the seamlines, and resew.
- If your seamlines meet, but at less than ¼", your seam allowances between the points were sewn at less than ¼". Go back and take a little wider seam allowance.
- If your seams meet, but cross at more than ¼", your seam allowances between the points were sewn at more than ¼". Sorry! It's time for a frog stitch (rip-it, rip-it, rip-it).

Match the two half stars together.

Center match with seamlines going in opposite directions. Three pins are used to match these three seamlines.

1. Pin No. 1 is a marking pin. Pin the center point by placing a pin into the point on the wrong side of one star half and through to the point on the right side of the other half.

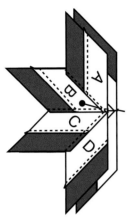

2. Hold the pin straight up and down through both points. Do not turn this pin.

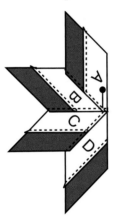

3. Pin No. 2 is used to hold the first set of diagonal seamlines together. While holding pin No. 1 upright, insert pin No. 2 following the diagonal seamline on both star halves. Pinning along the grainline (diagonal seamline) is more accurate than pinning off grain.

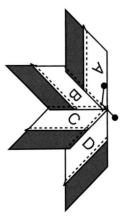

4. Pin No. 3 is used to hold the second set of diagonal seamlines together. Insert pin No. 3, following the other diagonal seamline on both star halves.

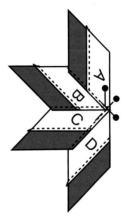

5. Now remove pin No. 1 (the upright marking pin).

Sew the two half-stars together.

1. Set your machine for a basting stitch (a long stitch).
If your points don't match on the first try, this basting stitch will be easy to rip out.
If your points do match, great! Set your machine for a regular stitch and resew over the basting stitch.

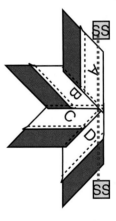

2. Starting with a Starter Scrap, sew the two half-stars together.

3. When you get a few stitches from the center point, remove the first pin. At the center point, the seamline must go through the exact point where the seamlines cross. If the point is slightly more or less than your seam allowance, sew directly over the point. Remove the second pin and continue sewing.

4. Set the center stitching line and press the center seam open.

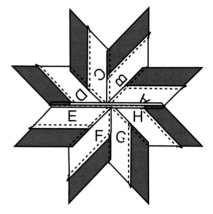

Matching Seams

In spite of all the accurate cutting, sewing, and pressing, some fabrics do not want to play together and match in the center, so I have some desperation matching techniques in Chapter 1. Try some of them when you are desperate.

Finish the stars

Sew interfacing to the stars.

1. Use lightweight interfacing or pattern tracing fabric to face the stars.

• For five-pointed stars, cut two 11" squares.

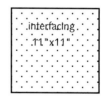

• For six-pointed stars, cut two 15" squares.

• For eight-pointed stars, cut two 18" squares.

2. Pin the interfacing square to the right side of each star.

3. Shorten the stitch length on your sewing machine. With the star on top, stitch around the entire star.

4. Trim the interfacing close to the stitching line outside the star. Clip to the stitching at the seamline between the inside points.

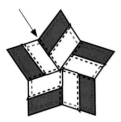

5. Cut a slit in the middle of the interfacing. Turn the star right-side out.

6. Press the star. The edges of the star now are finished, and the star is ready to appliqué to the background.

Sew the star to the background.

1. Cut background squares for each star.

• For five-pointed stars, cut two 10½" squares.

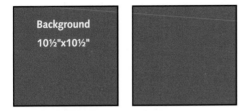

• For six-pointed stars, cut two 13" squares.

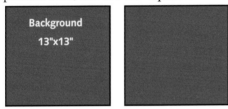

• For eight-pointed stars, cut two 15½" squares.

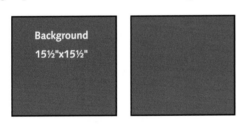

2. Fold and crease each square in half and then in half again to find the center.

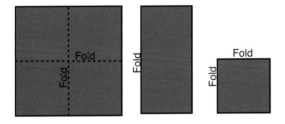

3. Center the star on the background by lining up the seamlines of the star with the creases. Pin the star carefully on the background. As an alternative to pinning, try using fabric spray adhesive.

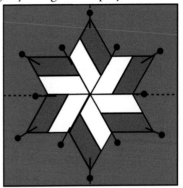

4. Use a hand or machine blanket stitch or blind hemstitch to sew the star to the background. Start stitching at an inside point. Most of the stitching should be on the background, very close to the edge of the star. The narrow bite that swings to the left should bite into the star.

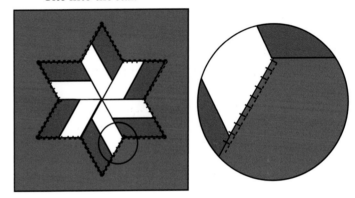

The top thread should be invisible, or it should match the background. The bobbin thread should match the background. If possible, set the machine needle to stop down in the fabric.

Sew border strips to the squares.

1. Cut border strips for each square.

- For five-pointed stars, cut four 4" wide border strips.

- For six-pointed stars, cut four 2½" border strips.

- For eight-pointed stars, cut four 1½" border strips.

2. Measure the width of each square. Cut two pieces from the border strip the exact width of the square. Sew the top and bottom borders to the squares with the strips underneath, so you can see the exact place to sew across the points of the star. The points of the star come right to the border strip.

New stitching lines are shown in white.

3. Set the seams. Press the seam allowances toward the border strip.

4. Measure the height of each square, including the top and bottom borders. Cut two pieces from the border strip the exact height of the square. Sew the side borders with the border strips underneath.

New stitching lines are shown in white.

5. Set the seams. Press the seam allowances toward the border strip.

Trim the squares.

Each of the background squares is a little larger than needed.

1. Fold and pin the square side to side to find the side-to-side center. Trim the side edges to measure 8½" from the fold.

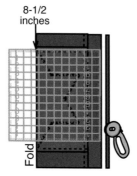

2. Fold and pin the square top to bottom to find the top-to-bottom center. Trim the top and bottom edges to measure 8½" from the fold. This should give you a 17" x 17" square.

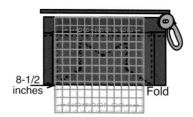

Sew the sashing strips to the blocks.

1. Cut 10 strips (3" x 42"/44") for the sashing and border strips.

2. From two of the sashing strips, cut three 3" x 17" pieces. Each row has two star squares and a vertical sashing strip.

3. Place the sashing strip on top and pin the beginning and end of the sashing strip to one star square in each row.

4. Start sewing with a Starter Scrap. Sew for 3" or 4" and STOP. Hold the pinned ends together and continue sewing.

5. Set the seams. Press the seam allowances toward the sashing strip.

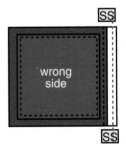

6. Sew the other side of the sashing strip to another star square, following the instructions above.

7. Set the seams. Press the seam allowances toward the sashing strip.

8. From four of the sashing strips, cut three 3" x 24" pieces for the horizontal sashing strips. (Measure the length of the rows, following the directions for measuring, cutting, and sewing long sashing strips for Emily's Quilt in Chapter 2.)

9. Sew the sashing strips to the top and bottom and in between each row.

10. Set the seams. Press the seam allowances toward the border strips.

Sew the side borders to the quilt top.

1. Use four of the 3" x 42" sashing strips. (Follow the directions for measuring, cutting, and sewing border strips in Chapter 2, Emily's Quilt.)

2. Set the seams. Press the seam allowances toward the border strips.

Finish the quilt.

1. Layer the backing, batting, and quilt top.

2. Machine or hand quilt.

3. Add the binding, referring to the directions on pages 140-142.

Chapter 6

Diamond Stars

Diamonds have always been used in quilts. Just follow my easy instructions for perfect stars made from diamonds.

Size: 23" x 26"

Hexagon Star Pillow

This six-pointed star pillow is made up of nine-patch blocks, created with the Starmaker 6 tool. Don't worry! If you don't have a Starmaker 6, you can use the template for the 6 angle on page 75.

Yardage:

⅛ yd. dark fabric for the star (green)
⅛ yd. light fabric for the star (peach)
1 yd. for the outside diamonds
28" x 28" piece of fabric for the backing
2 strips (2" x 42"/44") for the piping
3 yd. cord
Fiberfill

Sew strip sets.

1. Cut three strips (2½" x 42"/44") from each of the star fabrics.

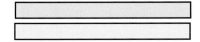

2. Mark a ruler at 2½" (the width of one strip) using tape or a piece of static sticker.

3. Sew three strips together (light/dark/light) to form strip set A. Sew three strips together (dark/light/dark) to form strip set B. Offset the strips by 2" to save fabric.

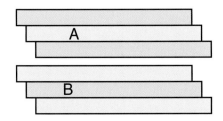

4. Set the seams. Press the seam allowances toward the darker fabric. (See Chapter 1 for directions on setting seams and pressing for accuracy.)

Cut the star segments.

1. Place the bottom of the Starmaker 6 along the bottom of the strip set. Cut the strip along the right-hand side of the Starmaker 6. Cut both A and B strip sets this way.

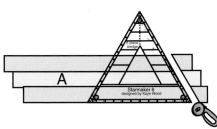

2. Place the ruler on the strip set so the mark on the ruler lines up with the cut end of the strip set.

3. Butt the Starmaker 6 up against the ruler. Make sure the bottom of the Starmaker 6 lines up with the bottom of the strip set.

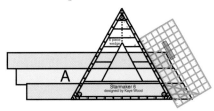

4. Remove the ruler and cut along the right-hand side of the Starmaker 6.

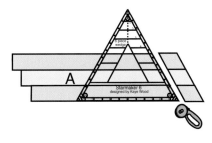

5. Cut 12 A segments (two for each star point). Cut six B segments (one for each star point).

Sew the first two segments.

Each star point is made up of two A segments and one B segment.

Match seamlines: Two different types of matching seamlines are used: a Needle Match and a 60-degree Match. No pins should be necessary to match these segments.

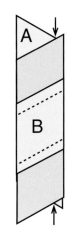

- A **Needle Match** is used for the V that forms at the top and bottom of the segments. (Complete directions are in Chapter 5, page 77, sewing techniques for six-pointed stars.) At the top and bottom, the two segments overlap. The stitching line starts and stops at the point they overlap.

1. Start sewing on a Starter Scrap (SS). Take a few stitches and STOP. As you come close to the first seamlines, finger pin the seamlines together using the 60-degree match.

A **60-Degree Match** will work for any 60 degree diamond, which is what you get when you cut with the Starmaker 6. No pins are needed.

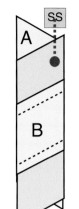

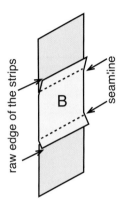

2. The first seam allowance on the B segment has been pressed toward the darker (green) fabric. To match the seamlines, temporarily bring the seam allowance down toward the lighter fabric.

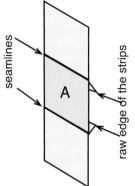

3. At the sewing edge of the fabric (the right-hand side), match the raw edge of the B segment to the seamline of the A segment. Finger pin to hold the seams in place.

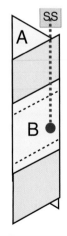

4. Just before stitching over this seam, release the seam allowance so it can go back toward the darker fabric. Sew almost to the next seam.

5. This second seam will match with the seam allowances lying as they were pressed. At the sewing edge of the fabric, match the raw edge of the top segment with the underneath seamline. Finger pin to hold the seams in place.

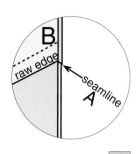

6. Sew to the end, and match the two segments where they overlap.

7. Chainstitch from one set to the next. Sew off the last set onto a Starter Scrap.

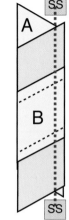

Sew the third segment.

1. Sew the third segment starting with a Starter Scrap. A V-shaped Needle Match is used at both the top and bottom of the stitching line. The 60-Degree Match is used on all the seams within the diamond point.

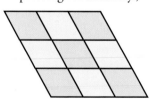

2. Set the seams. Press the seam allowances all to one side. (See Chapter 1 for information on pressing for accuracy.)

Kaye's Ripping Rule

Learn the technique before you rip. Rip and resew only once!

The 60-degree match can take some practice.

Keep on sewing. Do not rip until you match four points in a row. Then rip out the ones that don't match and resew. This way you will only have to resew once. If you rip and sew too many times in one place, you will distort and stretch the fabric.

Sew the points together into a star.

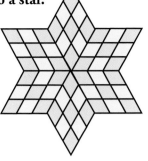

1. Follow the directions for sewing six-pointed stars on pages 76-79.

2. The seamlines between the diamonds will line up, and finger pinning can be used to match them.

Turn the star into a hexagon by adding outside diamonds.

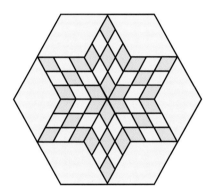

1. Mark the width of the strip set, approximately 6½", on a ruler using tape or a piece of static sticker.

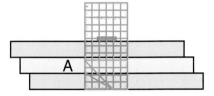

2. Cut two strips of the background fabric the same width as the strip set, approximately 6½" x 42"/44".

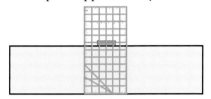

3. Place the bottom of the Starmaker 6 along the bottom of the strip. The 6 in a circle on the Starmaker 6 is at the bottom right-hand side of the strip.

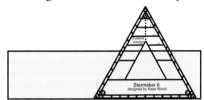

A Quilter Without A Country

One of our quilting cruises left from Aruba for the southern Caribbean. Bill and I flew to Miami to join Jane and Wayne Hill for a quilting cruise.

The next day we were to fly to Aruba when I realized I had my driver's license, but I had forgotten my passport, my birth certificate, etc. So I called and had my office fax me these documents.

We flew from Miami to Aruba on a charter the cruise line had arranged. Upon presenting my faxed documents to immigration in Aruba, the man looked at me and said, "These are not original documents." I said nothing, as I have learned is sometimes the best course of action, because it gives the person an opportunity to solve your problem for you.

He then said, "They seem to be on fax paper." Again I said nothing. "Where are the originals?" he asked. "At home," I replied.

My husband was sure they would not let me on the cruise ship, but what were their choices? Make me stay in Aruba, which is my favorite island, oh darn; fly me back to Miami; or allow me to board the cruise ship and become someone else's problem.

The immigration officer said, "You can't enter Aruba, but you can pass through to the ship. You should know that you probably won't be able to get back into the States. Only an American would travel with faxed documents." So they let us on the ship. I decided not to worry about getting back to the States until we returned from the cruise.

Twelve days later, after a great cruise, we flew back to Miami. The U.S. customs agent looked at my faxed documents. He said, "These are not the originals." I said nothing. He then said, "They seem to be on fax paper." Again I said nothing. "Where are the originals?" he asked. "At home," I replied. (Does this sound familiar?)

He then asked what immigration had said in Aruba. I told him they said, "Only an American would travel with faxed documents." The U.S. immigration man said, "He's probably right." And all ended well!

4. Cut the strip along the right-hand side of the Starmaker 6.

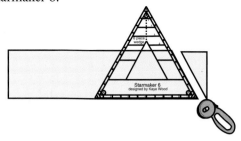

5. Place the ruler on the strip so the mark on the ruler lines up with the cut end of the strip.

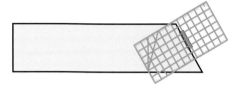

6. Butt the Starmaker 6 up against the ruler. Make sure the bottom of the Starmaker 6 lines up with the bottom of the strip.

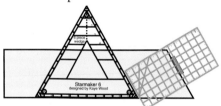

7. Remove the ruler and cut along the right-hand side of the Starmaker 6.

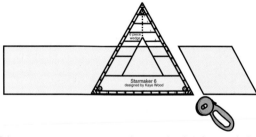

8. Continue cutting using the marked ruler and the Starmaker 6. Six diamonds are needed to complete the hexagon.

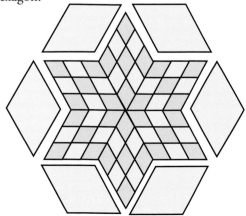

Add the outside diamonds.

The Infamous Y-seam

Don't cry over Y-seams! Just learn the secret.

The secret of an easy Y-seam: Anchor the seams between the star points by sewing all the way from top to bottom.

1. Place an outside diamond underneath a star diamond, right sides together. All sides and all angles of the outside diamond should line up with the star diamond.

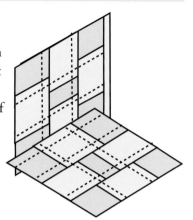

2. Start stitching on a Starter Scrap. Stitch the two diamonds together, starting at the top. Sew down to the seamline. Stop sewing with the needle down directly on the seamline between the two star diamonds.

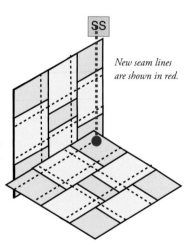

New seam lines are shown in red.

3. With the needle still down in the center of the seam allowance, fold the star diamond and line up the edge of the outside diamond with the second star diamond. Sew to the end and on to a Starter Scrap.

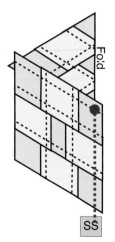

4. Press the seam allowances away from the outside diamond.

5. Sew all six outside diamonds to the star using this Y-seam technique.

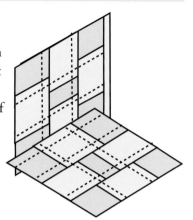

Piping

1. Cut two strips (2" x 42"/44") for the piping.

2. Sew the two piping strips together. Fold the strip, wrong sides together, around the cord. Sew through both folded layers of the piping close to the cord using a piping or zipper foot.

3. Sew the piping to the outside edge of the hexagon, right sides together. Use a piping foot or zipper foot on the sewing machine, and start sewing in the middle of one side.

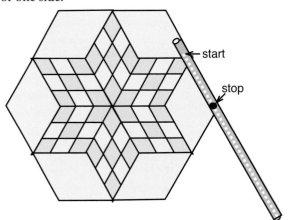

4. Sew to ¼" from the corner. With the needle down in the fabric, turn the hexagon to be ready to sew the next side.

5. Then, turn the piping to line it up with the next side of the hexagon (you may have to lift the presser foot to turn the piping).

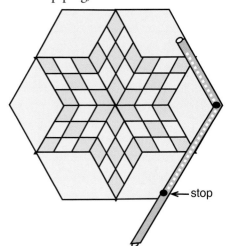

6. Continue sewing and overlap the end of the piping over the beginning at an angle toward the outside. Sew straight across the overlap.

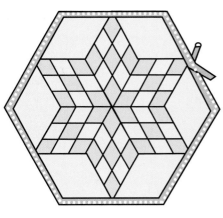

Finish the pillow.

1. Use the hexagon-shaped star as a pattern to cut out the backing and batting.

2. Layer the star and the backing, right sides together, with the batting underneath.

3. Using a piping or zipper foot, do an envelope style finish. (See the A Step Above Quilt on page 34.)

4. At each corner, clip the seam allowance of the piping down to the sewing line.

5. Turn the pillow, right-side out.

6. Stuff with fiberfill. Stitch the opening closed.

Size: 25½" x 25½"

Windowpane Star

This five-pointed star coordinates with the Windowpane Crib Quilt on page 56. They are both made from the same strip sets. The star is appliquéd to the background by stitching in the ditch through an accent strip. Make it into a matching wall hanging, or stuff it to make a pillow.

Yardage:

½ yd. light fabric for the star
½ yd. dark fabric for the star
¼ yd. for the accent strip
27" x 27" piece for the background
27" x 27" piece for the backing
27" x 27" piece of batting

Sew strip sets

1. Cut the following strips from the given fabrics:

Dark fabric:

Cut two 2¼" x 42"/44" strips.

Cut one 4¼" x 42"/44" strip.

Light fabric:

Cut one 2¼" x 42"/44" strip.

Cut two 4¼" x 42"/44" strips.

2. Sew Strip Sets A and B, alternating colors with the wide strip in the center, as shown. Offset the strips by 1½" to save fabric.

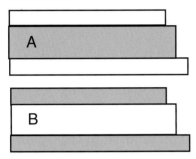

3. Set the seams. Press the seam allowances toward the darker fabric. (See Chapter 1 for directions on setting seams and pressing for accuracy.)

Cut the segments.

Place the bottom of the Starmaker 5 along the bottom of the strip set. Cut along the right-hand side of Starmaker 5.

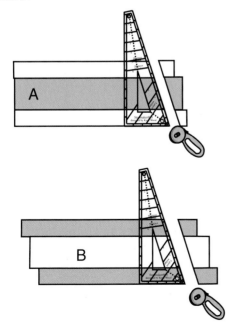

Wide Segments:

1. Mark a ruler at 4¼" (the width of the wide strip) using tape or a piece of static sticker.

2. Place the ruler on the A strip set so the mark on the ruler lines up with the cut end of the strip set.

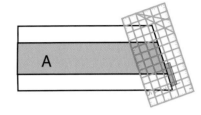

3. Butt the Starmaker 5 up against the ruler. Make sure the bottom of the Starmaker 5 lines up with the bottom of the strip.

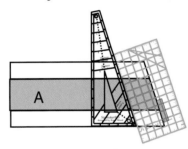

4. Remove the ruler and cut along the right-hand side of the Starmaker 5.

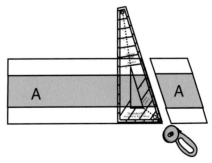

5. Cut five A segments (one for each star point). If you don't have a Starmaker 5, use the template for the 5 angle on page 70.

Narrow Segments:

1. Mark a ruler at 2¼" (the width of the narrow strip) using tape or a piece of static sticker.

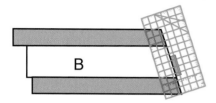

2. Place the ruler on the strip set so the mark on the ruler lines up with the cut end of the strip set.

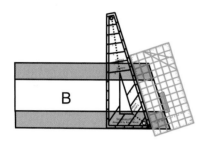

3. Butt the Starmaker 5 up against the ruler. Make sure the bottom of the Starmaker 5 lines up with the bottom of the strip.

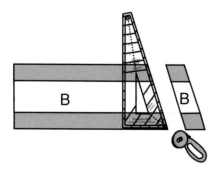

4. Remove the ruler and cut along the right-hand side of the Starmaker 5.

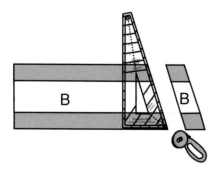

5. Cut 10 B segments (two for each star point).

Sew the star points together.

Each star point has two narrow B segments and one wide A segment.

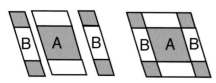

A diamond match is used on the seamlines between the diamonds, see the Lone Star Wallhanging on page 108. A needle match is used for the V that forms at the top and bottom of the segments, see page 77.

Cut accent strips

The accent strips are added to each point before they are sewn together into a star.

1. Cut three accent strips (1½" x 42"/44").

2. Cut these strips into 10 segments, each approximately 2" longer than each side of the star point.

Sew the first accent strip on each point.

1. Sew an accent strip to one outside edge of each star point, right sides together.

2. Fold and press the edge of the accent strip to the back, up and around the seam allowance.

New stitching lines are shown in white.

3. Pin the accent strip in place along the seamline.

4. Stitch in the ditch in the seamline between the star point and the accent strip.

5. Trim the ends of the accent strip by lining up a ruler with the edge of the star point.

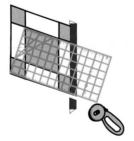

Sew the second accent strip on each point.

1. Fold and crease an accent strip in half, right sides together. This crease will be used to finish the point.

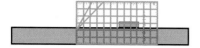

2. Leave a 1" extension at the top of the accent strip.

crease line

3. Sew the accent strip to the other outside edge of each star point, right sides together.

4. Bring the accent strip and the seam allowance away from the star point.

5. Fold this accent strip, right sides together, along the creaseline.

6. Shorten the stitch length to about eight stitches per inch. Sew the ends of the accent strip about 1/16" outside the angle. This will give you turning room.

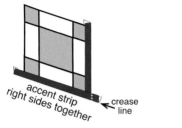

accent strip
right sides together
← crease line

7. Trim the excess seam allowance from the point. Turn the accent strip right-side out. The finished point will wrap around the end of the first accent strip.

8. Press and pin the accent strip under the star point.

9. Stitch in the ditch in the seamline between the star point and the accent strip.

Sew the star together.

Follow the directions for sewing five-pointed stars together on page 71-72. Use the diamond matching technique to match seamlines.

Finish the pillow.

1. Center the star on the background fabric.

2. Layer the star, the background, the batting, and the backing.

3. Pin the star in place.

4. Appliqué the star by stitching in the ditch in the seamline between the star and the accent strip through all layers.

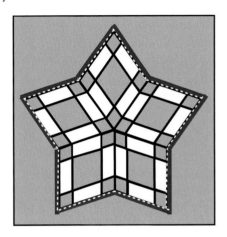

5. Machine or hand quilt.

6. For a wallhanging, add a sleeve (see page 110) and a binding (see page 140-142).

7. For a pillow, use an envelope finish (see page 34).

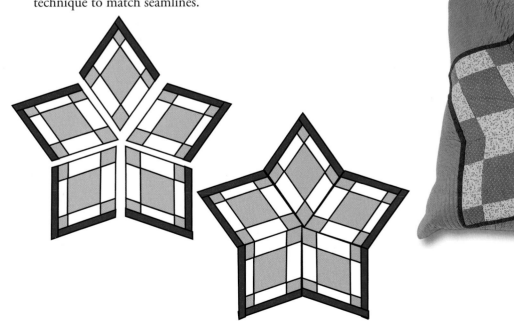

Holiday Table Drape

Make this drape in other seasonal fabrics for a year-round table decoration.

Yardage:

½ yd. red for the star
¼ yd. green for the star
½ yd. white for the star
1⅛ yd. for the lining

Sew the strip sets

1. Cut the given strips for the strip sets from each fabric listed below.

Red fabric:
Cut two strips (3" x 42"/44").
Cut one strip (5¼" x 42"/44").

Green fabric:
Cut two strips (3" x 42"/44").

White fabric:
Cut two strips (3" x 42"/44").
Cut two strips (5¼" x 42"/44").

2. Offset the strips by 3" to save fabric.

3. Sew one strip set A (narrow white/wide red/ narrow white) as shown.

4. Sew two strip sets B (narrow green/wide white/narrow red) as shown.

5. Set the seams. Press the seam allowances toward the darker fabric. (See Chapter 1 for directions on setting seams and pressing for accuracy.)

Cut the segments.

Place the bottom of the Starmaker 6 along the bottom of the strip set. Cut the strip along the right-hand side of the Starmaker 6.

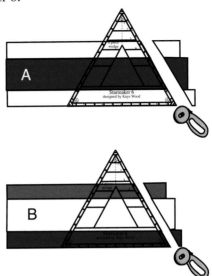

<u>Wide Segments:</u>

1. Mark a ruler at 5¼" (the width of the wide strip) using tape or a piece of static sticker.

2. Place the ruler on the strip set so the mark on the ruler lines up with the cut end of the strip set.

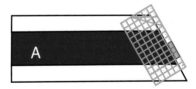

I'm Going Down With The Ship

One of the first events on any cruise is "the lifeboat drill." For those of you who still haven't cruised, this is what happens. The whistle blows (you have already been warned that this will happen). You are supposed to go calmly to your cabin, put on your life jacket, and go to your muster station (the place you will gather if the ship is in trouble). Now this sounds great when you know it is only a drill.

Something is wrong with this plan! Let me tell you how I think this will work if the ship is really in trouble. First of all, there are some cruisers who are still looking at the ship's map to find their cabin on the last day of the cruise. Will there be electricity to read the map if the ship is sinking?

Then they need to read the charts on the back of their cabin door because they don't remember where their muster stations are.

Most people spend their time at sea on deck or somewhere on the upper levels of the ship.

When the lifeboat bell rings, you can't use the elevators. To get to your cabin, you may have to climb down six or seven decks, get your life jacket, then climb up six or seven decks to get to your muster station.

Some of the quilters said, "The heck with that; I'd rather go down with the ship than climb seven flights of stairs."

A crew member told me, "There are enough life jackets in the lifeboats for everyone." So, it is quilters to the lifeboats; everyone else can try to find their cabins.

3. Butt the Starmaker 6 up against the ruler. Make sure the bottom of the Starmaker 6 lines up with the bottom of the strip set.

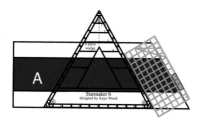

4. Remove the ruler and cut along the right-hand side of the Starmaker 6.

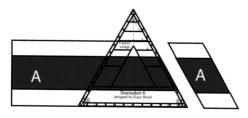

5. Cut six A segments (one for each star point).

Narrow segments:

1. Mark a ruler at 3" (the width of the narrow strip) using tape or a piece of static sticker.

2. Place the ruler on the B strip set so the mark on the ruler lines up with the cut end of the strip set.

3. Butt the Starmaker 6 up against the ruler. Make sure the bottom of the Starmaker 6 lines up with the bottom of the strip set.

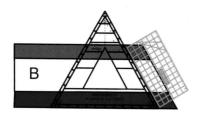

4. Remove the ruler and cut along the right-hand side of the Starmaker 6.

5. Cut 12 B segments (two for each star point).

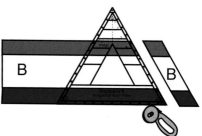

Sew the star points together.

Each star point is made up of one A segment and two B segments (one turned upside down).

Two different types of matching seamlines are used: a Needle Match and a 60-Degree Match. No pins should be necessary to match these segments.

A needle match is used for the V that forms at the top and bottom of the segments, see page 77.

As you come close to the first seams, use the 60-Degree Match, see page 94.

Sew the points together into a star.

Follow the directions for sewing six-pointed stars on page 76-78. The seamlines between the diamonds will line up and finger pinning can be used to match them.

Finish the table drape.

1. Pin the star to the lining fabric, right sides together.

2. Do an envelope-style finish, leaving part of one side open. Refer to A Step Above Quilt on page 34 for more information.)

3. Clip the seam allowance at the inside points almost to the seamline.

4. Trim the outside points and turn the star right side out through the opening.

5. Close the opening by hand or machine stitching.

Variation

1. Sew the diamonds together following the directions for the hexagon pillow on page 102, using a 60-Degree Match and Y-seam.

2. Pin the hexagon to the lining fabric, right sides together.

3. Do an envelope-style finish.

4. Turn the hexagon right-side out through the opening.

5. Close the opening by hand or machine stitching.

Shimmering Star Wall Hanging

The Lone Star is perhaps one of the best-known quilting patterns. It has eight points and can easily be strip-pieced, which means we will use the Starmaker 8 to cut the strip sets.

Yardage:

⅛ yd. fabric No. 1 (black floral)
¼ yd. fabric No. 2 (purple floral)
¼ yd. fabric No. 3 (dark peach floral)
⅓ yd. fabric No. 4 (medium peach floral)
¼ yd. fabric No. 5 (green solid)
¼ yd. fabric No. 6 (green floral)
⅛ yd. fabric No. 7 (light floral)
1¼ yd. for the background
¼ yd. for the borders
1⅓ yd. for the backing
40" x 40" piece of batting
¼ yd. for the binding

Cut the strips.

Cut the following strips (2½" x 42"/44"):
Fabric No. 1: one strip
Fabric No. 2: two strips
Fabric No. 3: three strips
Fabric No. 4: four strips
Fabric No. 5: three strips
Fabric No. 6: two strips
Fabric No. 7: one strip

Sew the strip sets.

1. Mark a ruler at 2½" (the width of one strip) using tape or a piece of static sticker.

2. Sew four strips together into each strip set as shown, offsetting each strip by 2". Off-setting the strips will save fabric.

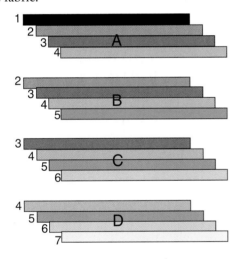

Notice that:
Strip set A uses strips No. 1 through No. 4.
Strip set B uses strips No. 2 through No. 5.
Strip set C uses strips No. 3 through No. 6.
Strip set D uses strips No. 4 through No. 7.

3. Set the seams. Press the seam allowances toward the darker fabric. (See Chapter 1 for directions on setting seams and pressing for accuracy.)

Cut the segments.

1. Place the bottom of the Starmaker 8 along the bottom of the strip set. The 8 in a circle on the Starmaker 8 is at the bottom right-hand side of the strip.

2. Cut the strip along the right-hand side of the Starmaker 8. (If you don't have a Starmaker 8, use the template for the 8 angle on page 82.)

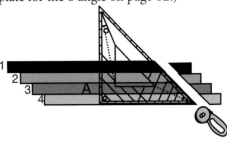

3. Place a ruler on the strip so the mark on the ruler lines up with the cut end of the strip set.

4. Butt the Starmaker 8 up against the ruler. Make sure the bottom of the Starmaker 8 lines up with the bottom of the strip.

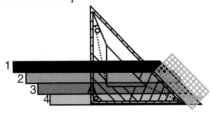

5. Remove the ruler and cut along the right-hand side of the Starmaker 8.

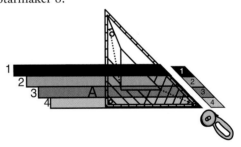

6. Cut eight segments from each strip set (one segment of each per star point) using the ruler for size and the Starmaker 8 for accurate angles.

Line up the segments.

Line up the segments in sets of the two that make up each diamond point. Two different types of matching seamlines are used: a diamond match and a V-shape match.

Diamond Match:

A diamond match is used on the seamlines (shown in circles) between the diamonds.

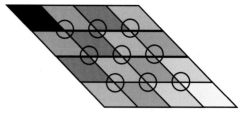

The seamlines must match ¼" in from the right-hand side of the segments (marked with •).

For each seamline that has to match:

1. Insert a pin from the wrong side of the top segment, directly in the seamline and ¼" from the edge.

2. Put the pin into the right side of the underneath segment, directly in the seamline and ¼" from the edge. Do NOT turn the pin now.

3. Hold the pin straight up and down through both points.

4. Hold the seam allowances together between your thumb and finger to keep the seamlines matched; then turn the pin and bring the point of the pin up through the fabric following the underneath seamline. **Note:** Pinning is more accurate when the pin goes along the straight of grain (along the seamline).

Needle Match:

A needle match is used for the V that forms at the top and bottom of the segments.

At the top and bottom, the two segments overlap. The stitching line starts and stops at the point they overlap. See page 77 for information on needle matching these segments.

Sew the segments.

1. Set the machine for a basting stitch. If your points don't match on the first try, this basting stitch will be easier to rip out. Start sewing on a Starter Scrap (SS).

2. Chainstitch the segment sets together, ending on a Starter Scrap.

3. Continue sewing segments together until the eight star points are finished.

4. Set the seams. Press the seam allowances all in one direction. (See Chapter 1 for directions on setting seams and pressing for accuracy.)

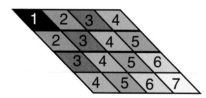

Accuracy Check

Fold the diamond diagonally. The corners should line up perfectly.

If the corners do not line up, re-measure, re-mark the strip set width on the ruler, and check the seam allowances.

The new seam in a diagram is shown in white.

Kaye's Ripping Rule

- Learn the technique before you rip. Rip and resew only once!
- This pinning technique can take some practice. Keep on sewing.
- Do not rip until you match four points in a row. Then rip out the ones that don't match and resew. This way you will only have to resew once. If you rip and sew too many times in one place, you will distort and stretch the fabric.

Sew the star.

1. Follow the directions for sewing eight-pointed stars on page 83-86.

2. Follow the directions for diamond matching on page 108.

3. Cut and sew the squares and triangles for the background pieces following the directions for the Starlight Quilt on page 126.

Mitered borders.

1. Cut four border strips (1½" x 42"/44").

2. For the top and bottom borders, measure across the width of the quilt, approximately 35½". (Refer to Emily's Quilt on page 15.)

Cut two of the strips this length plus 4", approximately 39½".

3. For the side borders, measure from the top to the bottom of the quilt, approximately 37½" (refer to Emily's Quilt on page 16).

Cut two of the strips this length plus 2", approximately 39½".

4. Pin the top and bottom border strips to the quilt, right sides together. There should be 2" extra at each end of the strip.

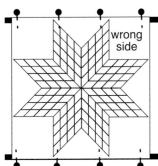

5. Start sewing at the edge of the quilt, and sew with the border strip underneath so you can see exactly where the seamlines form each point of the star. The points should be ¼" from the outside edge, but in case they are not, it is more important for the seamline to be exactly on the point. This seam is anchored (sewn all the way from one end to the next), which will make it easier to miter the border.

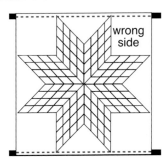

6. Press the seam allowances toward the border strips.

7. Pin the side borders so there is an overlap of 1" on each side.

8. Sew with the star on top, the border strip underneath. Start stitching at the seamline of the first border. Lock stitch and stitch to the seamline on the other end.

Start and stop at seamline

9. Press the seam allowances toward the border strip.

10. Overlap the ends of the borders. Trim the ends of the borders even with each other (this makes it easy to miter the corners).

11. At each corner, fold the quilt diagonally, right sides together.

12. Temporarily change the direction of the seam allowances at the corner so the seam allowances will go toward the star and you can see the seamline.

13. Line up the two borders. Match and pin at the outside edge and at the seamlines between the quilt and the borders.

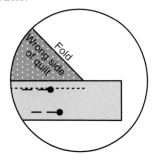

14. Fold the end of the top border strip diagonally and press to crease. This creased line is your stitching line.

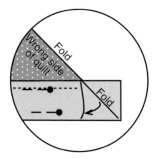

New stitching lines are shown in red.

15. Lock stitch at the seamline and sew diagonally to the corner, following the creased line.

16. Set the seams. Press the seam allowances in one direction. Trim off the excess fabric in the seam allowance.

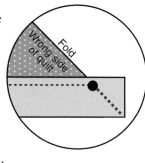

Finish the quilt.

1. Layer the quilt top, batting, and backing.

2. Hand or machine quilt.

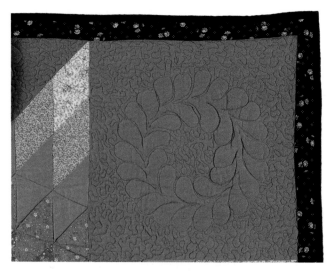

Add a hanging sleeve to the back.
A sleeve is added to the top back of a wall hanging so a dowel or a pole can be put through it to hang the quilt.

1. Cut a strip 8" wide and 2" shorter than the width of the quilt.

2. Finish the edges of this strip by folding and pressing under the edges ¼". Fold again and topstitch.

3. Fold and press the strip in half so it is now 4" wide.

4. Center the sleeve at the top of the quilt. Pin the raw edges to the top edges of the quilt. The sleeve should start and stop about 1½" from each side of the quilt.

5. Stitch the sleeve to the quilt with ⅛" seam allowance.

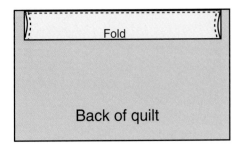

Fold

Back of quilt

Note: A wall hanging will hang straighter if you add a smaller sleeve to the bottom of the quilt. Use a dowel in this sleeve.

Add the binding.

Cut four binding strips (1⅝"). Sew the four strips together to make a binding strip that is long enough. See Chapter 8 for more information.

We Get Letters!

"Thanks for the great show. I'll continue to watch as long as it is good."

"As a pagan high priestess of my coven, I really appreciate the pentagon designs."

"I attended your seminars and learned a lot of wonderful tricks and tips that will make my quilting more enjoyable. You have such sensible techniques for beautiful results."

"Every Saturday morning I order a new book of yours. Give me a break! Get dull for awhile."

"I watch your show every week, but only after I go to church."

"Please send me all I need to know about Quilt In A Day Lap Strip Quilting. Is there a charge?"

"You make me glad I'm not a size 6."

All Cracked Up

My very first quilting TV series was taped in a real log cabin home that we "borrowed" for the shoot. During the taping, I started hearing cracking noises. You soon learn that most noises in the studio are not picked up on the mike, so you continue until the director stops the shoot. The cracking noises continued, and just as we finished taping the show, the large window above me shattered completely.

Thankfully, no one was hurt.

Life Begins To Revolve Around TV

One January, I slipped on the ice and broke all the bones and tore all the ligaments in my ankle. My first thought was, "Thank goodness we finished taping the series last week."

My first TV experience was in 1977. I taught some machine embroidery tips for five weeks on a local talk show. The hot lights dried out the cotton thread, and it started to fray and break. A quick solution was needed. We had to keep moisture in the thread, so we wet the whole spool. It worked great, but I watched water drip down the machine as I was sewing. Surprisingly enough, the machine continued to sew and nothing blew up.

As I cut pieces on TV, somehow I have to get rid of the unneeded fabric. A good friend of mine throws her fabric over her shoulder to get rid of it. I just push it on to the floor. But, pretty soon the pile of fabric pieces on the floor gets to be pretty deep. That can become a problem when I'm hard wired (my microphone is attached to a long cord). When I move from the sewing area to the pressing or cutting area, you can imagine how the microphone cord loops above and below the pile of fabric pieces, which makes the cord shorter and shorter.

On one show, the floor director crawled under the table and began to clear some of it out. Since he continually gave me a hard time (without reason), I just shifted my weight and came down on his hand. He started hitting my leg, thinking that I didn't know I was on his hand. And during all of this, I just continued to cut, press, and talk to all of you.

Like any other TV star, don't you think I should have a star on my dressing room door? You have to realize that most of the time the dressing room is also the bathroom. After whining to the same floor director about the star, I got to the studio only to find a small gold stick-on star (like they put on your papers in kindergarten) on the door. See, whining sometimes pays off.

I have a signal I give to my director that means "take a close up of something, because what I need next, I just dropped on the floor."

Chapter 7

More Stars

Now that the stars are sewn together, how are they finished into quilt blocks? There are many ways to finish stars, including several appliqué techniques and several piecing techniques. The appliqué techniques are the easiest, so I have started with these and progressed to the more difficult techniques.

Appliqué
(easiest method)

    This six-pointed star pillow is made up of nine-patch blocks, created with the Starmaker 6 tool. Don't worry! If you don't have a Starmaker 6, you can use the template for the 6 angle on page 75.

Finished Trim Appliqué

Note: Use a trim that is finished on both edges.

1. Center and pin the star carefully on the background. (An alternative to pinning is a fabric spray adhesive.)

2. Place the trim around the outside edges of the star, overlapping the edge of the star by ¼". The trim should be continuous with a fold at the inside and outside points.

3. Topstitch along both edges of the trim through all layers: the trim, the star, and the background.

Faced Finished Edges

1. Sew the star, right sides together, to a lightweight interfacing or pattern tracing fabric.

2. Turn the star right-side out and apply to the background with a machine blanket or appliqué stitch. (See complete directions on page 86.)

Trims That Are Sewn

Use this technique for trims, such as lace, rickrack, piping, narrow accent strips, etc.

1. Add the trim to the star before the star is put on the backing. Start sewing the trim to the star, right sides together, at an outside point.

2. Sew to the inside point, stopping on the seamline between the star points.

3. With the needle down in the seamline, bring the trim around to line up with the next edge of the star point. Continue sewing to the outside of the point.

4. Press the seam allowances toward the star. Cut this end of the trim even with the point of the star.

5. Leave about 1" of trim and start sewing at the next outside point at the edge of the trim. Sew to the inside point and continue as above.

6. At each outside point, fold the trim under the star.

7. Center and pin the star carefully on the background. (An alternative to pinning is a fabric spray adhesive.)

8. Stitch in the ditch between the star and the trim.

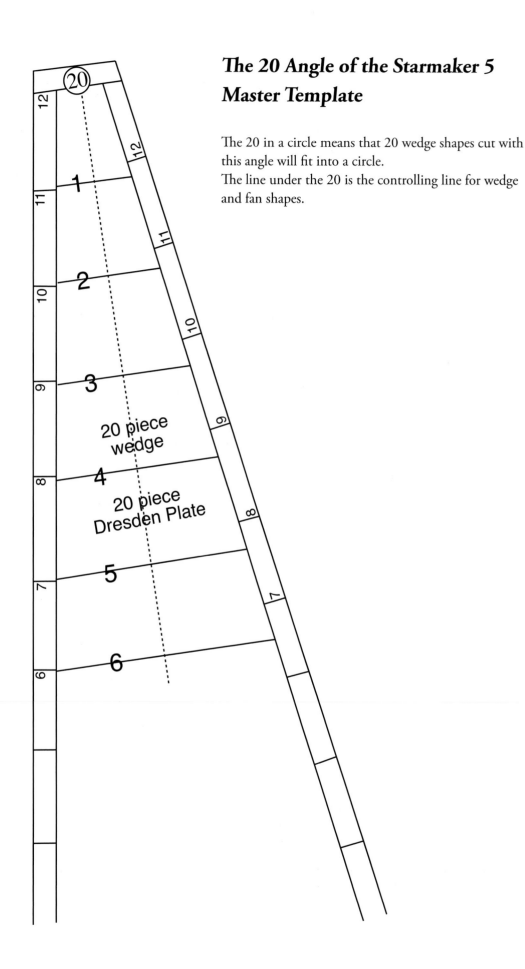

The 20 Angle of the Starmaker 5 Master Template

The 20 in a circle means that 20 wedge shapes cut with this angle will fit into a circle.

The line under the 20 is the controlling line for wedge and fan shapes.

20 piece wedge

20 piece Dresden Plate

Are You Really A Quilter?

In a crowded elevator, everyone got out except this elderly gentleman and me. He had a quilt badge on, so I knew he was part of the group.

"Do you really enjoy coming to quilt shows, or do you just get dragged along?"

He said, with a gleam in his eye, "Where else can I be in a room filled with women and lift up their skirts, look inside their jackets and vests, and they thank me for admiring their sewing?"

Elevators Only Go Up!

At the Hyatt Regency in Houston, we gather every year for the International Quilt Festival. There are two banks of elevators facing each other.

Many of us quilters were waiting on the ground floor for the elevators. When the elevator doors opened, a quilter next to me said, "Don't get in that elevator!" So I didn't.

"Why didn't we get in the elevator?" I wondered aloud.

"On this side the elevators don't go up," she replied.

I had to really think about this. "Where do these elevators go?" I asked.

"They only go down."

Are you as confused as I was? After all, we were on the ground floor. My next question seemed obvious, "How do we get to our rooms?"

"The elevators on the other side go up," was her quick reply.

So when one of them opened, we got in and went up.

I still am totally confused by this. Did she think the elevators go up, across and then down?

Hotel Rates

Late one night, in the middle of a blizzard and a whiteout, a friend and I finally found a hotel.

Since I'm the savvy traveller, I asked the desk clerk, "What's the cheapest rate?"

"One hour," he replied.

"What is the cheapest rate for all night?"

He said, "You want to stay the whole night?" while looking us over carefully.

Something sounded pretty strange to me. He said, "Do you really mean you just want a room for the night?"

"That's right."

He said, "Well I do have one room on the second floor."

We each had a large suitcase instead of an overnight case because we had not planned to stop. So I asked if there was an elevator. He said, "The stairs are over there."

"How do you accommodate handicapped people?" I inquired.

"Lady, we don't get handicapped people here."

"Do you have a bellman to help us carry the luggage up the steps?"

He said, "Most people don't bring luggage here."

Believe me, if the wind was not howling and the snow was not coming down in a blizzard, we would have left.

"We'll take the room, and we'll carry our own luggage."

He said, "Good idea; but lock the door and put a chair under the knob, and don't come out of the room regardless of what you hear."

So we did!

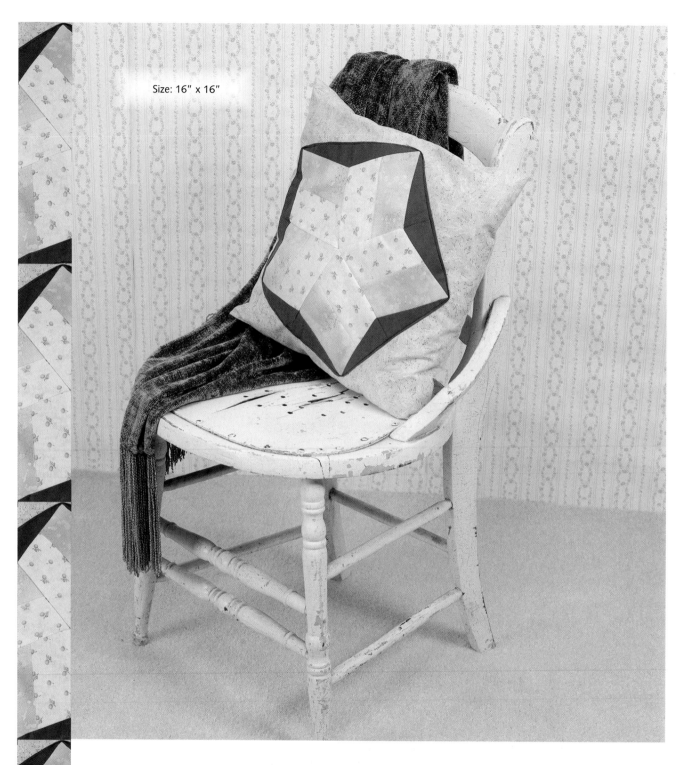

Size: 16" x 16"

Pentagon Star Pillow

The easiest way to square up the five-pointed star is to first sew it into a pentagon, then appliqué it to a square.

The Starmaker 5 was used to cut the diamonds for the five-pointed star, so it will also cut the accurate wedge shapes that fill in around the star.

Yardage:

⅛ yd. dark fabric for the stars
⅛ yd. light fabric for the stars
¼ yd. for the wedges of the pentagon
18" x 18" for the background
18" x 18" for the backing
Fiberfill or pillow form

Make the star.

1. Cut one 2½" x 42"/44" strip from each of the star fabrics.

2. Sew the strips into a strip set, following the directions on page 68.

3. Mark the width of the strip set (approximately 4½") on a ruler using tape or a piece of static sticker.

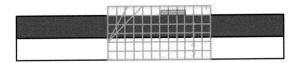

4. Cut the strip set following the directions on page 68.

Note: There are two ways to turn the star into a pentagon:
• Single wedge (seamed):
Sew a wedge to two sides of each star point before sewing the star points together.
OR
• Double wedge (not seamed):
Sew a double wedge between each star point after the points are sewn together.

<u>Single Wedge</u>

Cut single wedges.

1. Cut the strip for the wedges the same measurement, approximately 4½". If your strip set measures more or less than 4½", use your measurement.

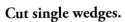

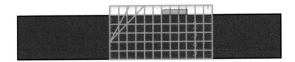

2. Fold and press the strip in half end to end, wrong sides together. The folded strip still will measure the same as in Step 1.

3. Trim off the right-hand side of the strip to straighten the edge and to remove the selvedges.

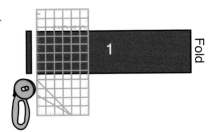

4. Place the Starmaker 5 on the strip with the line under the 20 touching the top of the strip at the left-hand side.

5. Cut along the right-hand side of the Starmaker 5 to get a wedge shape. The No. 1 wedge is cut from the top layer; the No. 2 wedge, a mirror image, is cut from the bottom layer.

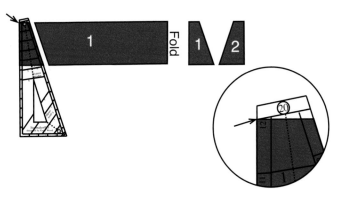

6. Turn the Starmaker 5 upside down. The line under the 20 should touch the bottom of the strip at the right-hand side.

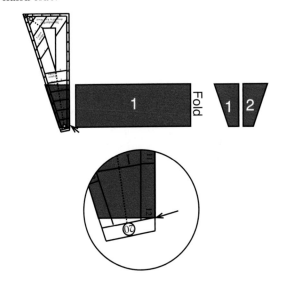

7. Cut five No. 1 and five No. 2 wedges for each star.

Sew the No. 1 wedges to the star points.

1. Sew a No. 1 wedge, right sides together, to one outside edge of each of the star points. Start stitching on a Starter Scrap, matching seams with a needle match (see page 77).

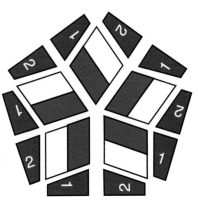

2. At the bottom of each piece the pieces should overlap exactly at the seamline. Sew off onto a Starter Scrap.

3. Set the seams. Press the seam allowances toward the wedge shapes. The top and bottom of each wedge should line up with the sides of the star point.

New seamlines are shown in red.

Sew the No. 2 wedges to star points.

1. Sew a No. 2 wedge, right sides together, to each of the other outside edges of the star points. Start stitching on a Starter Scrap.

2. There is a needle match only at the top of each piece. There is no match at the bottom of each piece. Just sew to the end of the No. 1 piece and chainstitch to the next piece.

3. Set the seams. Press the seam allowances toward the wedge shapes.

Sew the points of the star together.

1. Follow the directions for sewing five-pointed stars together on page 71-72.

2. Finger pin or pin to match the seamlines between the points and the wedges.

3. Set the seams. Press the seam allowances toward the wedge shapes.

4. Trim to ¼" away from the star points.

<u>Double Wedge</u>

Cut the double wedges.

1. Measure the width of the strip or strip set used to cut the points of the star. It should measure approximately 4½".

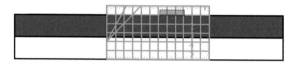

2. Cut the strip for the wedges double the above measurement, approximately 9" wide.

3. Fold and press the strip in half top to bottom, wrong sides together. The folded strip will measure the same as in Step 1.

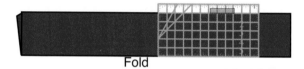
Fold

4. Straighten the edge and remove the selvedges.

5. Place the Starmaker 5 on the strip with the line under the 20 touching the top of the strip at the left hand side.

6. Cut along the right-hand side of the Starmaker 5 to get a wedge shape. When opened, the wedge will be doubled.

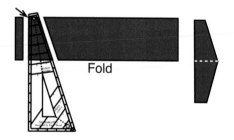
Fold

7. Flip the Starmaker 5 over so the line under the 20 touches at the top of the strip at the right-hand side. Cut on both sides of the Starmaker 5.

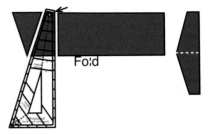

Sew the double wedges to the star.

1. Sew the star together, following the instructions on page 71-72.

2. Line up a wedge under one of the star points.

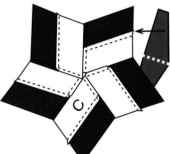

3. Pin into the seamline on the star, through to the creaseline on the double wedge, and back up through the seamline between the points of the star.

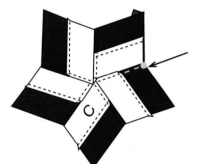

4. Sew with the star point on top. This is sewn like the Y-seam (see page 96). Start sewing with a Starter Scrap and do a needle match (see page 77).

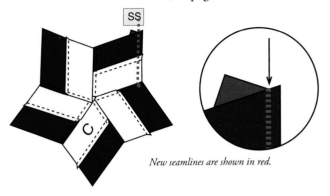

New seamlines are shown in red.

5. Stop with the needle down in the seamline between the star points.

6. With the needle still down on the seamline, pull the other edge of the double wedge even with the second side of the star. Sew off the end onto a Starter Scrap.

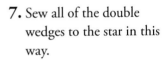

7. Sew all of the double wedges to the star in this way.

8. Press the seam allowances toward the star.

9. The pentagon can be appliquéd to a square using any of the appliqué techniques (see page 114).

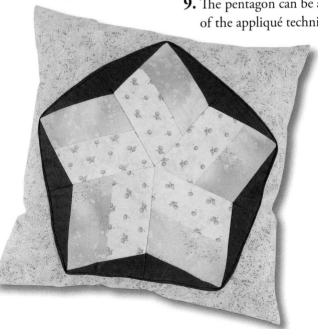

Size: 33" x 52"

Starlight Quilt

This lap quilt using eight-pointed stars with pieced backgrounds is just the right size for the back of your couch. Snuggle under it on a cold night.

Yardage:

¼ yd. dark fabric for stripped diamonds
¼ yd. medium fabric for stripped diamonds
¼ yd. light for stripped diamonds
¼ yd. for large diamonds
1 yd. for background squares
1 yd. for sashing and first border
⅔ yd. for second border
40" x 60" for backing
40" x 60" piece of batting
⅓ yd. for binding

Sew the strip sets.

1. Cut three strips (1½") from the dark, medium, and light fabrics.

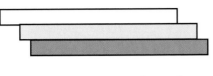

2. Sew three strip sets, each with a dark, medium, and light strip.

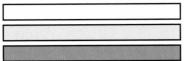

Sew the strips with right sides together; offset each strip by 1½" to save fabric.

3. Set the seams. Press the seam allowances toward the darkest fabric. (See Chapter 1 for setting seams and pressing accurately.)

Cut and sew strips for large diamonds.

1. Mark the width of the entire strip set on a ruler using tape or a piece of static sticker. It should be approximately 3½".

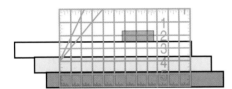

Accuracy Tip

This is the measurement used to cut the strip into diamonds.

2. Using the large diamond fabric, cut three strips the width of the strip set measurement.

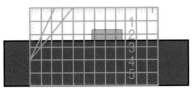

3. Sew the strip set and the wide large diamond strip, right sides together, along the right-hand side.

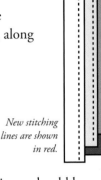

New stitching lines are shown in red.

Cut the diamond segments.

1. The seam between the strip and strip set should be at the bottom. Place the bottom of the Starmaker 8 along the bottom of the strip and strip set.

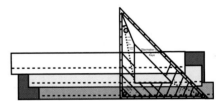

I Said Six

A friend and I were in an elevator that had two sets of call buttons. My friend was in front of one set of buttons. Another person came in to the elevator and said, "Sixth floor."

Before this person had a chance to push the six, my friend pushed the six button in front of her. This person then said, "This elevator must be voice activated."

We didn't tell her what had happened. So if you are ever in an elevator and someone enters and talks to the buttons, it might be the same person.

2. Cut along the right-hand side of the Starmaker 8. (If you don't have a Starmaker 8, use the template for the 8 angle of the Starmaker 8 on page 82.)

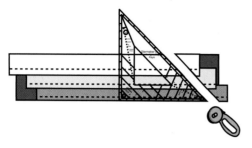

3. Place a ruler on the strip so the mark on the ruler lines up with the cut end of the strip set.

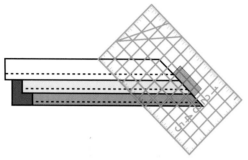

4. Butt the Starmaker 8 up against the ruler. Make sure the bottom of the Starmaker 8 lines up with the bottom of the strip.

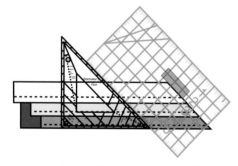

5. Remove the ruler and cut along the right-hand side of the Starmaker 8. This will give you two diamonds that are already sewn together with anchored seamlines.

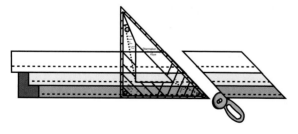

6. Cut four double diamonds for each star (a total of 24 double diamonds), using the ruler for size and the Starmaker 8 for accurate angles.

7. Set the seams. Press the seam allowances toward the large diamond (away from the pieced diamond).

Sew the star.

1. Sew two double diamonds, right sides together, into half stars, following the instructions for sewing eight-pointed stars on page 83-86, with one exception. Because every other diamond has cross seams, press these seams away from the pieced diamonds to reduce the bulk in the seam allowance.

2. From the right side, the point that has to match is ¼" from the edge.

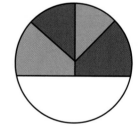

3. Sew the two half stars together, matching the center points.

4. Set the seams. Press the center seam open to reduce bulk.

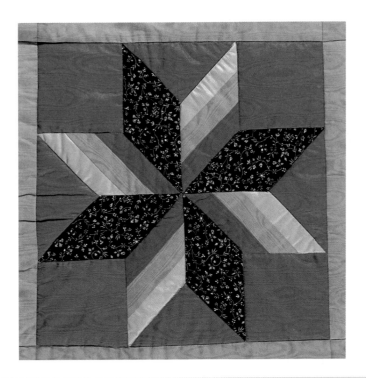

Want To Get Your Quilt Noticed?

Make A Bad Quilt!

I like to watch people who are looking at quilts. When they look at a good quilt, they take a good look and go on to the next one.

But, if the quilt is bad, they study it and call their friends over to look at it, too. Possibly, they are trying to figure out why they don't like the quilt, and yet, it is still hanging at the show, so it must be a "good" quilt.

If you want to try this, hang a "bad" quilt at a quilt show and watch what happens.

Sorry, No Rotary Cutters For You

Our company policy is that if you have a number after your name, we will not ship rotary cutters or blades to you!

My TV show, "Kaye's Quilting Friends," is really popular in prison, and the prisoners love to order rotary cutters and blades.

According to the letters we get, we could eliminate all that money spent on prisons because most of the letter-writers are innocent.

One man told us he was convicted of tax evasion, but that it was his brother-in-law's fault.

He said he was sentenced to 24 months, had already served 19, and had seven more months to go.

If he had only had a calculator, maybe he wouldn't have tried to evade his taxes ... and he might even know when his sentence was up!

Squaring Up Eight-Pointed Stars: Sewing Techniques

Four corner squares and four triangles are used to square up the star. The grain line of each piece should go in the same direction (up and down in the block). This will help to keep your quilt block square.

<u>Corner Squares</u>

Cut and mark the squares.

1. Measure the width of the entire strip set used for the star diamonds. It should be approximately 3½".

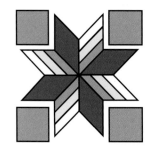

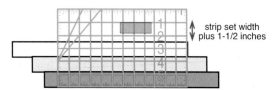

2. Add 1½" to this measurement and mark it on a ruler using tape or a piece of static sticker.

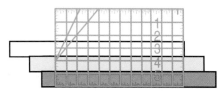

strip set width plus 1-1/2 inches

Starlight Quilt: This measurement will be approximately 5" (3½" plus 1½").

Confetti Star Pillow (page 132): This measurement will be approximately 6" (4½" plus 1½").

3. Cut strips using the measurement in Step 2.

Starlight Quilt: Cut three strips (5" x 42"/44") from the background fabric.

Confetti Star Pillow: Cut one strip (6" x 25") from the background fabric.

4. Cut these strips into squares.

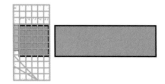

Starlight Quilt: Cut 24 squares (5").
Confetti Star Pillow: Cut four squares (6").

5. Mark the top of each square with a pin.

> ## Accuracy Tip
> The pins will help you to keep the grain lines going in the same direction.

Line up the edges and sew the seam.

1. Place the squares in the corners of the star. The pins should be at the top in each corner.

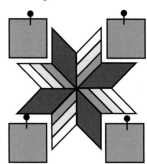

2. Crease-mark the squares. Fold and crease the squares, right sides together, so the diagonal crease lines up with the seamline between the points of the star. These crease marks will help to line up the squares with the points of the star.

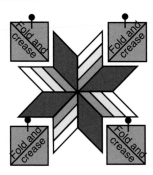

3. Place a square, right sides together, under the star point, with the right-hand sides lined up.

4. Insert a pin into the seamline between the star points, exactly ¼" from the edge. The pin should go through to the square and come out on the creased line.

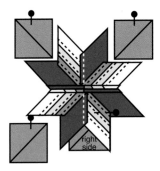

5. Bring the point of the pin up through the square and back up into the star point at right angles to the sides. From the back, the pin in the square will look like this:

6. Sew the square to the point, starting at the pin (on the seamline ¼" from the edge). Lock stitch (see Chapter 1) on the seamline and sew to the end.

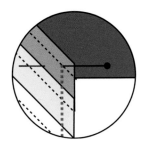

New stitching lines are shown in red.

Note: The bottom edges will not line up because the square was cut slightly larger than needed so the star block can be trimmed later.

7. Press the seam allowances toward the star.

Sew the second side of the square.

1. Fold the star, right sides together.

2. Line up the side of the square with the other side of the star point.

3. Place a pin through the starting point (in the crease lined up with the first seam). Check to make sure all the fabric is out of the way.

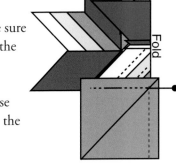

4. Lock stitch at the crease and sew all the way to the edge.

5. Press the seam allowances toward the star. Do NOT trim the edges. They will be trimmed after the triangles are added.

Triangles

To keep the quilt block square, it is best if the outside edges of each triangle are cut on the straight of grain of the fabric. To do this, first cut a fabric square and then cut the square into four triangles.

Trim and mark the fabric.

1. Measure the width of the entire strip set used for the star diamonds. It should be approximately 3½".

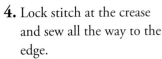

2. Add 2" to this measurement; double this and mark it on a ruler using tape or a piece of static sticker.

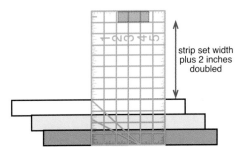

strip set width plus 2 inches doubled

Starlight Quilt: This measurement will be approximately 11" (3½" + 2" = 5½" x 2 = 11").

Confetti Star Pillow: This measurement will be approximately 13" (4½" + 2" = 6½" x 2 = 13).

If your star point measures more or less than the above example, use your measurement.

3. Take the rest of the background fabric and trim the top and left-hand side to straighten the edges and remove the selvedges.

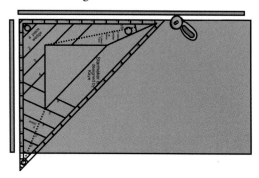

Tip

An easy way to trim the fabric is to place the Starmaker 8 about ½" to ¾" away from the top and left-hand side of the fabric.

4. Turn the Starmaker 8 so the bottom of it lines up with the top of the fabric. The 8 angle of the Starmaker 8 should be in the upper left corner.

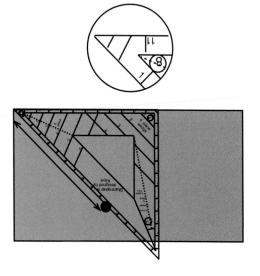

5. Using the measurement from Step 2, place a mark along the diagonal edge of the Starmaker 8.

Starlight Quilt: Make a mark at 11".
Pinwheel Star Pillow: Make a mark at 13".

Cut the square into triangles.

1. Slide the Starmaker 8 over so the right-hand edge lines up with the mark.

2. Cut along the right-hand side of the Starmaker 8 from the top of the fabric down to the mark.

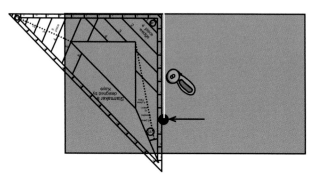

3. Turn the Starmaker 8 so the 4 angle is at the mark.

4. Cut along the bottom of the Starmaker 8. This will give you the size square needed.

Starlight Quilt: **Pinwheel Star Pillow:**
Cut six squares.   Cut one square.

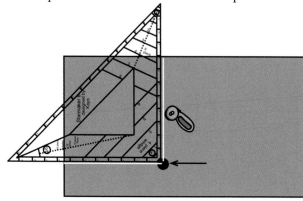

5. Cut the square diagonally from corner to corner using the Starmaker 8.

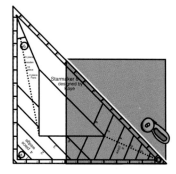

6. Turn the Starmaker 8 to cut the square diagonally in the opposite direction. This will give you the four triangles needed for one star square.

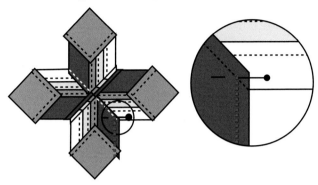

Place the triangles in position.

1. Mark the triangles with A, B, C, and D with self-stick notes.

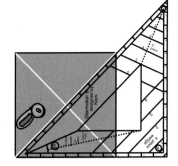

2. Crease-mark the triangle: Fold and crease the triangles, right sides together, from the point to the center of the side. These crease marks will help to line up the triangles with the points of the star.

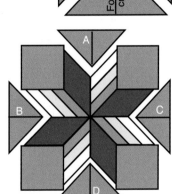

3. Place the triangles in position. The straight of grain will be on the outside edge of the triangles. The crease line lines up with the seamlines between the star points.

Sew the first seam.

1. Place a triangle, right sides together, under the star point with the right-hand sides lined up.

2. Insert a pin into the seamline between the star points exactly ¼" from the edge. The pin should go through to the triangle and come out on the creased line of the triangle.

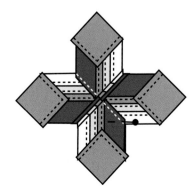

3. Bring the point of the pin up through the triangle and into the star point at right angles to the sides.

4. Sew the triangle to the point, starting at the pin (on the seamline ¼" from the edge). Sew all the way to the outside edge of the star point.

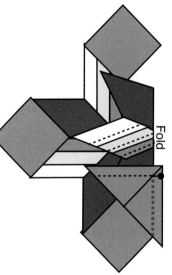

5. The seam allowance of the square should be laying toward the star point. Sew over it so it stays in the direction it was pressed.

Sew the second side of the triangle.

1. Fold the star, right sides together.

2. Line up the side of the triangle with the other side of the star point.

3. Place a pin through the starting point (in the crease lined up with the first seam). Check to make sure all the fabric is out of the way.

4. Lock stitch at the crease and sew all the way to the edge.

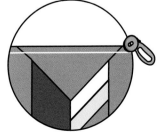

5. Press the seam allowances toward the star.

6. Trim each side of the star block ¼" beyond the points of the star.

Add the sashing strips and borders.

1. Cut two strips (3") for the short sashing strips.

2. Sew a sashing strip to the right-hand side of three of the quilt blocks. (Follow the directions on page 61 for measuring the block and for cutting, sewing, and pressing the sashing strips.)

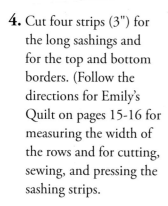

3. Sew a block to the other side of each short sashing strip to complete each row.

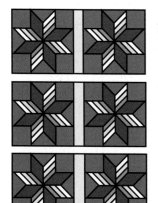

4. Cut four strips (3") for the long sashings and for the top and bottom borders. (Follow the directions for Emily's Quilt on pages 15-16 for measuring the width of the rows and for cutting, sewing, and pressing the sashing strips.

5. Cut four strips (3") for the side borders.

6. Sew two together for each border. (Follow the directions for Emily's Quilt on pages 15-16 for measuring the length of the quilt and for cutting and sewing the border strips.)

To assemble and add the second borders, follow the directions for the first borders.

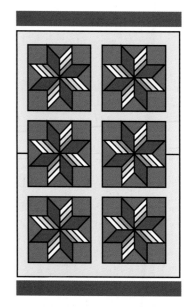

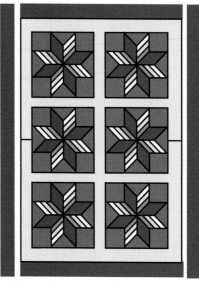

Finish the quilt.

1. Layer, quilt, and bind the quilt following the directions in Chapter 8.

by Brenda Jonsson
Size: 23" x 23"

Confetti Star Pillow

This pillow is created with the same eight-pointed star as the Starlight Quilt on page 122. It is a companion to the Confetti Pinwheel Quilt on page 40.

Yardage:

1 yd. dark fabric for the stars, piping, and backing
½ yd. light fabric for the stars and border
½ yd. for the background
3 yd. cord for piping
Fiberfill

Sew strip sets.

1. Cut two strips (2½" x 42"/44") from each of the star fabrics.

2. Sew two strip sets, offsetting the strips by 2½".

3. Set the seams. Press the seam allowances toward the darker fabric.

Make the star.

1. Follow the directions on the previous pages for making an eight-pointed pinwheel star.

2. Add background squares and triangles to the star, following directions for the Starlight Quilt on page 118.

Make the pillow top.

1. Cut two strips (2" x 42"/44") for the top and bottom borders.

2. Cut two strips (2" x 42"/44") for the side borders.

3. Follow the directions for measuring border strips in Emily's Quilt (page 15-16).

4. If desired, place batting and backing under the pillow top. Machine or hand quilt.

Piping

1. Cut three strips (1" x 42"/44").

2. Sew the strips together to make one long strip.

3. Fold the strip, wrong sides together.

4. Place the cord inside the fold.

5. Sew with a piping or zipper foot close to the cord.

6. Sew the piping to the right side of the star, raw edges together. Lap the end of the cord over the beginning at an angle toward the outside and sew straight across the overlap. (Complete directions for sewing piping are included in the hexagon shaped pillow on pages 96-97.)

Finish the pillow.

Finish with an envelope-style finish, referring to the directions on page 34.

Chapter 8

Finishing Touches

Your project never really is finished until it is bordered, quilted, and bound. This chapter will help you through the finishing process.

Borders

When does a quilt require a border, and what is a border supposed to do? Should the border be darker or lighter than the quilt? Should it repeat fabric already used in the quilt? How wide should the border be?

First of all, forget the "shoulds." It is your quilt, and it should only do what you want it to do.

• Does your quilt even want a border?

Let the quilt tell you if it needs a border. Does the quilt look finished without a border? Yes, well great, forget a border, and your quilt top is finished.

• Why do we add borders to a quilt?

We add borders for a variety of reasons: to frame the quilt the way we frame a photo; to keep the design of the quilt from moving off the quilt; to make the quilt larger; to add more fabrics; and to provide a place to show off your quilting stitches.

If a border isn't needed to do one or more of these things, don't add a border.

• Is it better to have a light or dark border?

It depends on what the quilt wants. My quilts take over and make a lot of these decisions for me. Two borders, one light and one dark, might add a lot of depth to your quilt. Borders also can be pieced so you could include several shades of dark and light.

The border fabric does not have to repeat a fabric used in the quilt. Sometimes the border is the most important part of the quilt, but only let that happen if you want it to happen.

Stripes can be really effective in borders. Cut them with the stripe or across the stripe.

• How wide should the borders be?

As a rule, try borders that are no wider than about one-third of the individual blocks, unless the border fabric tells you it wants to be wider, e.g., a certain print that looks better cut wider. If your quilt needs wider borders, try using two or more narrow borders.

Borders need to be cut the exact length of the quilt top. See Emily's Quilt, pages 15-16, for measuring, cutting, pinning, and sewing border strips with square corners.

For mitered borders, see the Shimmering Star wall hanging on page 110.

Layering

Layering is the term given to the process of putting quilt, backing, and batting together.

Cut the backing and batting approximately 4" larger than the finished top. The backing should be held taut by using a quilt frame or by taping the fabric, right-side down, to a flat surface, such as the floor or a pingpong table. The batting is laid on top of the backing. Smooth the batting out, but don't stretch it. The quilt top is placed right side up over the batting.

The three layers can be held together with a fabric spray adhesive, safety pin basting, or hand basting.

Finishing Techniques

Eyelet Finish
See the Precious Patches Quilt on page 50.

Envelope Finish
For potholders, see the Pinwheel Pot Holders on page 38.

For quilts, see the A Step Above Quilt on page 34.

Piping Finish
See the Hexagon Star Pillow on page 92.

Hanging Tab
For potholders, see the Pinwheel Pot Holders on page 38.

Hanging Sleeve
A sleeve is added on the top, and sometimes also on the bottom, of a quilt so it can be hung.
See the Shimmering Star wall hanging on page 110.

Quilting

Quilts may be quilted by hand or machine. Or they may be tied by hand or machine, see the Precious Patches Quilt on page 51.

Thank goodness for professional quilting machines. I'm an OK machine quilter, but my quilts deserve better. So mine are all sent out to be quilted.

Machine quilting takes a lot of practice, but these tips might help you:
- Use an even-feed foot.
- Lock your stitches.
- Use matching thread, decorative thread, or invisible thread in the needle.
- The bobbin thread should match the backing fabric or coordinate with it.
- Bring the bobbin thread to the top of the quilt. Hold both the bobbin and top thread and start quilting.

Try a sample before starting on your quilt. Good practice projects are the Rail Fence Place Mats on page 24.

Bindings

A binding finishes off the edges and frames the quilt.

The back of the quilt can be wrapped around to the front to form a binding. See Emily's Quilt on pages 17-18.

Or a separate binding strip can be sewn to the quilt. It can be cut on the straight of grain or on the bias. I prefer a straight-of-grain double binding.

The finished binding width (the width showing on the quilt top) can be very narrow to extra wide.

Your quilt—your choice.

But, the seam allowance must be the same width as the finished binding. If the finished binding is ½", then the seam allowance must be ½" because the binding must be padded with the edge of the quilt.

For a double binding, cut the binding strip six times the finished width of the binding; i.e., if the finished width is ½", the strips would be cut 3" wide.

The one exception to the binding strip being six times the finished width is when the finished binding is ¼". Then the strip needs to be cut 1¾" to allow for the turn of the cloth.

Teaching Seminars

My quilts usually are in suitcases, ready to go with me when I do seminars or teach classes. Only once, thank goodness, did I open the suitcase and find I had brought quilts for a seminar that was different from the one scheduled.

So I did the only thing I could do. I taught the seminar that included the quilts in the suitcase. At the end, I just couldn't resist telling the audience what had happened. Several of them said they didn't think I was teaching what was scheduled, but it was OK and they learned a lot.

Many years ago, prior to a quilt show, the person in charge called me and said only two people had signed up for my class. "Why do you suppose that is?" she asked.

"I don't have a clue."

Then she said, "Did you know that when I took the program to the printer I only had 15 pages with me. There were supposed to be 16, but we were short of time, so we printed the program with only 15 pages. The page that was missing was the information about your class."

That should have been a clue to her why my classes did not do well. I'd like to know how two people signed up when I wasn't in the program.

At this same show, there was a "meet the teacher" event. Guess what? This event was also on "my" page, so no one knew about it. So only the 10 teachers were there. And you'll never believe what came next. The director carried on, complete with microphone, as if the room was completely full (maybe her eyesight was bad). She welcomed everyone (all 10 of us) and then we had to introduce ourselves, complete with microphone, to everyone present (all 10 of us). Keep in mind that we all travel and teach and each of us could have introduced any one of the 10 of us.

And we all did it with a straight face.

Bind your project.

1. Cut enough binding strips to go around the quilt, plus 12".

2. Sew two or more binding strips together on the diagonal or bias. Trim the excess seam allowance.

3. Press the seam allowances open.

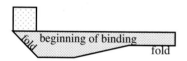

4. At the beginning of the strip, fold the end diagonally and press a crease.

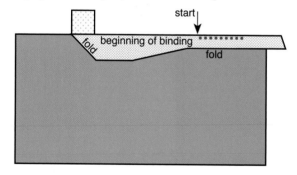

5. Fold the binding in half, wrong sides together, and press. See the Windowpane Crib Quilt on page 56 for my QuickFold technique.

6. Leave a 6" tail at the beginning of the binding. Start sewing on one side of the quilt with the raw edges of the binding strip even with the edge of the quilt top.

7. After mitering the last corner (perfect mitered corners are shown on page 142), stop stitching. Lay the beginning creased fold and the ending of the binding strip together. Fold a crease in the ending.

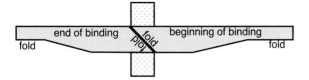

end of binding   beginning of binding
fold   fold   fold
fold fold

8. Bring the folded crease lines together, right sides together, pin and sew.

9. Finish sewing the binding strip to the quilt.

10. Bring the binding strip around to the back of the quilt and hand stitch it in place. The corners will miter perfectly on the front and back of the quilt.

I'm A Celebrity! Adiós Reality!

Apparently having my own show on TV makes me a celebrity, but thank goodness it is only within the quilting world.

Outside of quilting, many of my friends don't really know what I do, other than I am gone a lot. Some think my staff makes quilts; in reality, they answer phones, take orders, pack and ship orders, maintain our Web site, accompany me, staff our booth at consumer and trade shows, and produce my television show.

In the small town in which we live, I am usually known as Dr. Wood's wife; my husband is a retired high school principal. At quilt shows, he is known as my husband.

My workday consists of eight to 10 hours of writing instructions and designing and making samples for books and TV. That is if I feel like working. If not, I don't.

Our grandchildren call my TV show "Grandma movies." I guess they think every grandma is on TV.

It does mean that my teaching schedule is now filled years ahead, and I am endorsing quilting and sewing products. But some fun things have happened because of it.

At a consumer show, a quilter ran into my booth and said, "I know who you are."
"Hi, I'm Kaye Wood."
"No, that's not right," she said as she turned and left the booth.

At an airport check-in, I was fumbling to find my driver's license. The agent said "You don't need an ID." When did this change? I wondered to myself.
He continued, "I know you. I watch your TV show all the time."
Then the security officer next to the agent said, "Please step aside; we need to dump search your luggage."
"OK, but why?" I inquired.
"You meet one of the profiles."
It did not seem prudent to argue with security people, but, I thought, is the suspected terrorist a short, overweight grandmother who doesn't need an ID?

When flying to present a seminar for a guild, before 9-11, I often was met at the gate by someone from a quilt guild.
A woman said to me "Hi, Kaye."
"Hi, how are you?" I replied.
Instead of going to the baggage claim, we stood and talked at the gate, which I thought was strange. After a few minutes, she said "Well, I have to go catch my plane." She wasn't there to meet me, but just saw me and stopped to chat.
I continued to the baggage claim area and met the quilt guild representative. Now I make sure I have the name and phone number of the quilter who I am supposed to meet.

Mitered Bindings
Perfect mitered corners can be sewn on any shape quilt.

1. Start sewing along one long edge. Stop a seam allowance from the next edge. Turn the quilt and sew diagonally to the corner.

2. Fold the binding strip up so it lines up with the next side of the quilt.

3. Fold the binding strip down and start sewing at the top edge of the quilt, and a seam allowance in from the side.

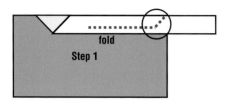

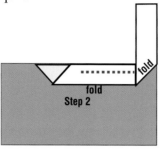

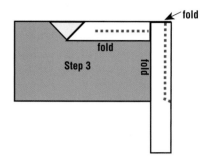

Squares and Rectangles

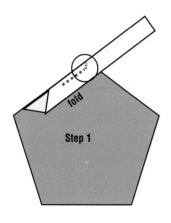

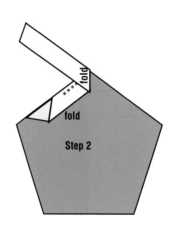

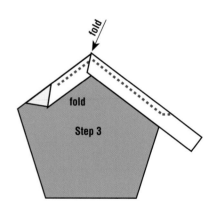

Pentagons

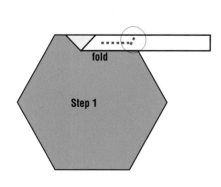

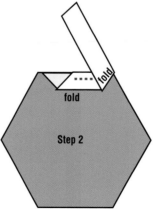

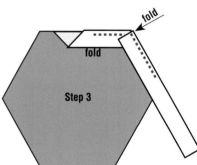

Hexagons

Flying Is Good For A Laugh

Flying from Michigan to Phoenix, the John Wayne-type pilot came on and told us, in his smooth, I-am-in-control voice, that one of our engines was smoking, and he would have to shut it down. He also said that he had to shut the engine down on the opposite side so we would stay level. That made sense to me.

He smoothly explained that when he did this, it would feel like we were momentarily flying backward, but that we would have no problem flying with the two remaining engines. And it happened exactly the way he said it would.

Soon, JW came on the PA and said one of the remaining engines was starting to cause problems so he was going to have to shut it down. He sounded so much in control that no one seemed to panic, because he was in charge and he said, "No problem." Where have I heard "No problem" before?

The way I figured, he was also going to have to shut down both remaining engines and two from the two remaining engines doesn't leave you with much.

Then JW said we were going to land in Kansas City and they were looking for another aircraft for us. Where do you look for an aircraft? You either have one or you don't.

In the meantime, they offered us free drinks.

I fly a lot. My advice is that when they offer you free drinks, take them.

After a short time in Kansas City, we were on our way with JW to Phoenix. And every one of us got back on the plane.

A short time later, JW came on the speaker and said we had to slow down and take it easy going into Phoenix because a military plane without landing gear was making an emergency landing and that it would be a good opportunity for us to see how it looks from the air when they foam the runway. Boy, was he smooth! I just knew that foam was for us. We circled the field, and it was interesting, but then we did see the military plane land.

Now do you really think JW was as calm and in control as we all thought he was?

Caribbean Outfit

All of one cruise was spent shopping for an outfit for my lecture on how to dress "appropriately" for a cruise.

I close my seminars with one of my Caribbean outfits, and I'd like to share my Caribbean sunset with you.

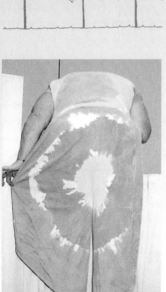

Kaye Wood is my name!
Stripping is my game!

My *Strip Like A Pro* program includes Strip Quilting books, videos,
Starmaker Master Templates, and View & Do Shapes

Starmaker Books:

Quilt Like A Pro • Turn Me Over—I'm Reversible •
Serger Patchwork Projects • Starmaker Ablaze I—Log Cabin Triangles •
Starmakers Ablaze 2—Log Cabin Diamonds •
Savage Star Pattern • Six-Hour Quilt book and video •
Twin Star Jacket • Stardust Quilt •
Strip Quilting Projects (books 1 thru 10) • Easy Hexagon Designs book and video •
Fantastic Fans and Wedge Designs book and video • Strip Cut Quilts book and video
• Stars Made Simple

Starmaker Master Template Set

Starmaker 5 • Starmaker 6 • Starmaker 8
Starmaker Design Concepts book and video

Other Books:

Six-Hour Quilt

View & Do Books

Pieces of Eight • Circles Made Simple • Stars Made Simple

View & Do Shapes

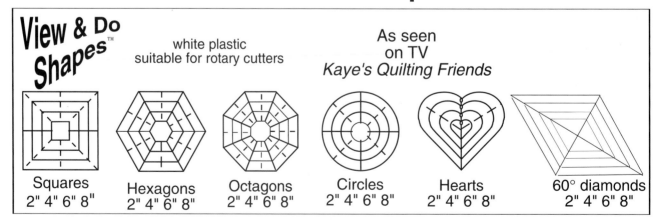

View & Do Shapes™

white plastic
suitable for rotary cutters

As seen
on TV
Kaye's Quilting Friends

Squares
2" 4" 6" 8"

Hexagons
2" 4" 6" 8"

Octagons
2" 4" 6" 8"

Circles
2" 4" 6" 8"

Hearts
2" 4" 6" 8"

60° diamonds
2" 4" 6" 8"

Kaye Wood, Inc.
PO Box 456, West Branch, MI 48661
1-800-248-KAYE (5293)
www.kayewood.com
kayewood@kayewood.com